Praise for
Break Open the Sky

"Rarely do I read something with such deep spiritual analysis, profound insight, and poetic storytelling as Stephan Bauman's new book *Break Open the Sky*. For those who think they already know the good news of Christ but still long for more, this short, honest, and beautifully written book is what you have been waiting for. *Break Open the Sky* is a timeless contribution to Christian and human spirituality."

—KEN WYTSMA, president of Kilns College, founder of The Justice Conference, and the author of *The Grand Paradox: The Messiness of Life, the Mystery of God and the Necessity of Faith*

"We live in a brave new world where terrorism, racism, and bigotry drive an engine of fear in our society and within our churches. Bauman tackles these topics head-on, compelling us by God's love and exciting us by his grace to reject fear, embrace risk, and rediscover faith to care for people in the shadows. *Break Open the Sky* is a much-needed and valuable work that speaks to our current landscape in a fresh, new way."

—ED STETZER, Billy Graham Distinguished Endowed Chair for Church, Mission, and Evangelism, Wheaton College

"A journey not for the faint of heart, *Break Open the Sky* is an invitation to live out an authentic faith in the midst of fear . . . , an invitation to hope!"

—TOM LIN, president and CEO of InterVarsity Christian Fellowship

"Humanitarian Stephan Bauman has witnessed love conquering fears, but he has also seen fear stymie faith's best intentions. His lessons from his life of global service can help us shed our fears and reawaken our commitments to that 'sociological impossibility,' the global Christian community."

—DAVID NEFF, former editor in chief of *Christianity Today* (retired)

"In uncertain and anxious times, *Break Open the Sky* is a critically important book for those who want not just to survive but to thrive. It is for those who want to find joy and power and impact in any season, especially the challenging ones. This is must reading for anyone who wants to go deeper into God and deeper into the real world we live in. This book couldn't be more timely."

—REV. BILL HALEY, executive director of Coracle

"In the tumultuous days we are living in, when fear seems to be overtaking the hearts of so many, Stephan Bauman's *Break Open the Sky* comes like a torch in the darkness. This book amplifies the very good news of an upside-down kingdom and is a clarion call to live out a faith that is honest, gritty, and beautiful."

—ROB MORRIS, president and cofounder of Love146

"Stephan has been an eyewitness to real fear factors that have disrupted lives and derailed nations. With this book Stephan delivers a rich treasure trove of personalities and stories accumulated in his journey through this globe's minefield of violence, disaster, and disregard. This book is an entertaining and thought-provoking travel guide offering a way to joy in the midst of insecurity."

—STEVE HAAS, catalyst, World Vision

"Stephan Bauman's artistry with words puts a new lens on old truths and a new way to view the events of our day that leave me feeling encouraged and courageous. This book is a must read for individuals, small groups, and university classes who truly want to live as God's peculiar people—fearless when the world says to be fearful, seeing abundance when the world cleaves to its storehouses of wealth, seeing 'the other' as the ones who Jesus calls us to reach out to, especially now."

—DR. BETH BIRMINGHAM, senior director of Leadership and Staff Development, Compassion International; Associate Faculty, Eastern University

"Stephan Bauman is a unique mix of visionary, poet, strategist, and pastoral leader. *Break Open the Sky* is a book of hope in a world gripped by a culture of fear. Hope is out there. It may be messy and raw, but it's glorious. Life isn't about living with an absence of fear; it's about taking the risk to love anyway. Stephan points to a deeper understanding of the nature of God, one that he's witnessed firsthand in countless stories from around the world."

—MARK AND VICKIE REDDY, The Justice Conference

BREAK
OPEN
THE
SKY

BREAK OPEN THE SKY

SAVING OUR FAITH
FROM A CULTURE OF FEAR

STEPHAN BAUMAN

MULTNOMAH

BREAK OPEN THE SKY

Italics in Scripture quotations reflect the author's added emphasis.

Details in some anecdotes and stories have been changed to protect the identities of the persons involved.

Trade Paperback ISBN 978-1-60142-585-0
eBook ISBN 978-1-60142-587-4

Cover design by Kristopher K. Orr

Published in the United States by Multnomah, an imprint of the Crown Publishing Group, a division of Penguin Random House LLC, New York.

MULTNOMAH® and its mountain colophon are registered trademarks of Penguin Random House LLC.

The Cataloging-in-Publication Data is on file with the Library of Congress.

Printed in the United States of America
2017—First Edition

10 9 8 7 6 5 4 3 2 1

SPECIAL SALES
Most Multnomah books are available at special quantity discounts when purchased in bulk by corporations, organizations, and special-interest groups. Custom imprinting or excerpting can also be done to fit special needs. For information, please e-mail specialmarketscms @penguinrandomhouse.com or call 1-800-603-7051.

To all those who awaken and
astonish from the edge.
You are my teachers.

We are not trapped or locked up
in these bones.
No, no. We are free to change.
And love changes us.
And if we can love one another,
we can break open the sky.

—Walter Mosley

There is no fear in love.

—John, the disciple of Jesus

Contents

Disillusioned

You cannot swim for new horizons until you
have courage to lose sight of the shore.

—William Faulkner

A few days before Christmas in 2015, the sound of bullets striking steel forced a passenger bus in northeastern Kenya to
screech to a halt. A group of ten militants from al-Shabaab, a Somali
terrorist group, stormed the bus. With guns pointed they asked the
passengers to identify their religious affiliation—Muslim or Christian. Their intention was to kill the Christians. Only a year before,
terrorists had boarded a similar bus and executed twenty-eight non-
Muslim passengers.[1]

But the passengers refused to comply. Instead, Muslims gave their
fellow Christian travelers religious attire so they wouldn't be identified.
Then they told the terrorists "to kill them together or leave them alone."[2]
"We stuck together tightly," said one Muslim passenger. "The militants

threatened to shoot us, but we still refused and protected our brothers and sisters" until the attackers "gave up and left."[3]

Somehow this story slipped by us mostly unnoticed. Maybe it was the holiday rush or the excitement over the release of the latest Star Wars film. Or maybe we couldn't take another story about terrorism after the attacks in Paris and San Bernardino. Or maybe we just didn't like the story. Amid the growing animosity toward refugees, it seemed inconceivable that a group of Muslims would protect their Christian "brothers and sisters" from certain death.

Last year while I was visiting a seminary in New England, a first-year student asked me why she "experienced more love outside the church than within." Christian discourse seemed to mirror the vitriol of the national debate, where perspectives are polarized and racism and xenophobia are thinly veiled. Within her own community a growing undercurrent of fear troubled her. Hesitant in tone and demeanor and careful not to blame or judge anyone, she wondered what had become of the faith community she loved so much. How could so many people denounce immigrants, refugees, or Muslims yet still profess to follow the One who asks us to love not only the "least of these" but our enemies as well?[4]

Data seems to support our friend's angst. When it comes to what happens in our country today, more than 40 percent of Americans "believe that people of faith (42%) and religion (46%) are part of the problem."[5]

Faith, it seems, has a branding problem.

Meanwhile, anxiety in the United States has reached epidemic levels.[6] "We are living in the most fearmongering time in human history," said Barry Glassner, a leading sociologist and author of *The Culture of*

Fear. "There's a lot of power and money available to individuals and organizations who can perpetuate these fears."[7] And when it comes to racial tension, 84 percent of adults agree "there is a lot of anger and hostility between different ethnic and racial groups in America."[8]

But maybe our fears are justified. After all, we live in precarious times. The magnitude of suffering we witness on the global stage—whether from acute acts of terrorism, chronic violence, or sudden injustice—invites a torrent of fear and raises a thousand questions. An avalanche of opinions proffered daily by news outlets, radio talk shows, and social media leaves us feeling threadbare, disillusioned, and even nauseous at times. We are perplexed, torn between principle and what seems practical, between love and safety, and between faith and fear. We are ready to support needed policy but not at the expense of character. We grieve the loss of life in Syria, Yemen, and South Sudan. We want to honor the heritage of our country by welcoming the "huddled masses yearning to breathe free,"[9] yet our actions as a nation seem to undermine the very virtues we so passionately profess.

How do we honestly grapple with legitimate questions about faith in the face of such tangible fear? Can we muster enough courage to calm our trepidatious souls long enough to clearly consider what is at stake, not only for us, but also for our children, nephews, nieces, and grandchildren as well?

When Muslims identify with Christians, offering their lives to protect them—whether motivated by their faith, sense of humanity, or social context—we encounter a profound phenomenon, a beautiful collision so stark, so rare, so astonishing that it forces us to ask why our faith, on the whole, is not producing a similar or better version of such sacrificial love? Is the God of the universe reckless enough to showcase

an extraordinary deed by a people considered by many to be our enemies in order to challenge, awaken, or maybe even shock us? Could this
same God require in us a love so breathtaking, so intrusive, so astonishing that our initial reaction might be to scurry away, taking theological
cover from such a formidable mandate?

What does it really mean to follow Jesus in the face of so much
fear?

By now you might be thinking this is a book about how to become
better people. We should fear less, love more, give sacrificially, and so
on. Or it may sound as if I am giving instructions for pulling ourselves
up by our bootstraps so we can become postmodern good Samaritans
who welcome the stranger, feed the hungry, and clothe the naked.[10]
While such actions can be helpful, I am not interested in outlining an
ethic or defending a ready-made position. We don't need a new rising to
justice that ultimately loses its steam or a deeper leaning into the better
angels of our nature. The issues we face—the fear of terrorism, the
fracturing of society, the superficiality of faith—point to something
much deeper. Our disillusionment is symptomatic of something fundamental to our identity as people of faith. There are ruptures in the core
beliefs that may have sheltered us for too long. Our faith is not simply
adrift. We may actually be shipwrecked and in need of rescue.

If you are disillusioned or feel done with it all, if you feel angry,
exhausted, bored, grieved, or apathetic, I humbly suggest that now
might be the time to take a risk. Be warned (or maybe reassured): the
answers we seek will not be found on the left or right of the political
spectrum. I am convinced Jesus was neither a conservative nor a liberal.
While he cared deeply about people, culture, justice, and, yes, even

politics, he was, and still is, something altogether different. It's this different way—a less-traveled path, paved with a surprising ethic and powered by an astonishing love—that I am after.

You might be searching for the same. It's dangerous to settle for something less than what we hoped for.

We must hold out for the real thing.

A FELLOWSHIP OF FEAR

The hallmark of our times—in our politics, our social discourse, and increasingly, our faith—is fear. Often subtle but also brazen at times, fear is becoming so commonplace we assume it's normal. We are more afraid than we realize.

There is certainly no shortage of things to fear today. According to one survey, government corruption, cyberterrorism, tracking of personal information, terrorist attacks, biowarfare, identity theft, and economic collapse top the list of things we fear most.[11] Incredibly, a recent poll found that more Americans were afraid in 2014 than just after the September 11 attacks in 2001.[12] Three out of four Americans believe "occasional terrorism" is now part and parcel of our way of life,[13] even as a majority of Americans have favored banning Muslims from entering the United States.[14]

Yet by almost any standard we are better off today than ever before in history. When Franklin Roosevelt spoke his famous words "the only thing we have to fear is fear itself," the nation's banks were collapsing, one in four workers was unemployed, and Adolf Hitler had just become chancellor of Germany.[15] Global life expectancy was about forty-five years then.[16] Today it's about seventy.[17] In 1900, in some American cities, as many as 30 percent of children died before they were a year old. Today it's less than 1 percent in the United States and less than 5 percent globally.[18] The majority of the world's population then lived in extreme poverty. Today? Less than 15 percent.[19]

We live longer, hurt less, and earn more. Yet somehow we are more afraid than we used to be.

Fear is popular today because it's profitable. Producers of media in all its forms have become merchants of fear, stoking fires of controversy, threat, or angst in search of larger audiences. Politicians, both conservative and progressive, traffic in fear to secure support and shore up votes. Corporations employ fear to make us buy more of their products. Friends warn us of the latest health scare, food allergy, or crime epidemic. Even religion, as an enterprise, makes use of fear.

Fear often masquerades as frustration, anger, anxiety, or apathy. So much of what we experience—from rage on the highway to the buried frustration in our hearts, from the drive to achieve greatness to the drudgery of daily life, from flare-ups in the office to put-downs—is rooted in fear. When we ask ourselves what's wrong—what's *really* wrong—if we are honest, we admit we are afraid of failure or success or love or rejection or hurt.

Fear slips surreptitiously into our souls, producing anger, an unexpected edginess, or just a vague anxiety. Sometimes we don't even know why we feel the way we do. We may even wonder if we are becoming what we fear most. All this leaves us feeling vulnerable, even distraught at times.

We live in a culture of fear.

I AM DISILLUSIONED TOO

My wife, Belinda, and I are no strangers to faith. For more than two decades, we immersed ourselves in a broad spectrum of church and parachurch life. Our lives were indelibly marked during these years. Our passion for the world was birthed and then matured. We discovered lifelong friends. Our children were born. We wouldn't trade these experiences for anything. We have no regrets, only gratitude.

But we, too, are increasingly disillusioned. Why is everyone so afraid? Not long ago on an otherwise normal day, after a barrage of unfounded angst about the global refugee crisis, I said to Belinda, "If this is what it means to follow Jesus, I want out." Like the young woman we met on that seminary visit, we grieved the political and fear-laden discourse coming from various faith communities.

Belinda and I began to see the degree to which the church we had fallen in love with seemed bent on serving itself as its members clamored to join an "inner ring,"[20] distinguished by being affiliated with certain people and brands, by wielding influence and power, or by espousing certain theological perspectives, all the while ignoring "the least of these." The idea we had given our lives for—that the church "exists for the benefit of those who are not its members"[21]—began to seem increasingly questionable, if not altogether implausible. Faith felt more like an exclusive club than a covenant community.[22]

Today, along with the many authentic expressions of worship and the genuine hearts we encounter so often in the greater community of faith, we still experience the dark underbelly of Christian culture. Self-promotion, judgment, and gossip are too common, usually subtle, and often camouflaged with mentions of Scripture, theology, or well-intentioned promises to pray. Dissension within the body of Christ seems epidemic. Friendships too often come to an abrupt end. People leave churches and organizations wounded, many surprised by their painful journey.

I recognize that offering critique is fraught with peril. Generalizations are dangerous, delicate, and prone to be misunderstood. I grieve my own participation in these subtle sins and have asked colleagues, friends, and family members for forgiveness on many occasions. I pray my words will be received not as a gavel of judgment but as a scalpel of healing. My intention isn't simply to expose our common problems but to offer a helping hand so we may lift ourselves to a better place. Yet doing so requires us to name and accept the current state of affairs.

I am convinced that much of what we call faith is really not faith at all; instead it's a culture that has developed around faith. More broadly, I am concerned our version of Christianity has become, in part, only an echo of the real thing, an industry feeding off a caricature of religion. Economic drivers—sales, financial growth, or funding, for example—rather than inspired vision tend to set the priorities. Social media "Likes" determine prestige and popularity. Talent and pedigree are preferred over character. Success is measured by numbers, followers, or donations rather than impact.

All these elements can work together to foster values and practices that undermine the very things we believe in and long for. Humility is exchanged for popularity. Power is wielded in unhelpful ways, often unknowingly. Compassion becomes a badge of honor rather than a form of altruism. Put simply, when we are afraid, we are more likely to compromise what's most important to us—our convictions about faith, character, or even the nature of truth. We are especially susceptible when we are offered some form of real or perceived security in exchange for compromising our faith.

Too often leaders, politicians, public officials, and even preachers and pastors exploit fear to their advantage. We don't have to reach too far back in history for examples that prove this is true. Consider the rise of Fascism in the 1930s, the Red Scare in the early 1950s, or even "radical Islamic terrorism" today. "It is far safer to be feared than loved," said Niccolo Machiavelli[23] in referring to the benefits of manipulating with fear.

I believe these subtle—and not so subtle—mistakes are symptoms of a deeper problem. Our problems are not necessarily rooted in faulty theology, cults of personality, external threats, media manipulation, or even capitulation to secular culture. Our problems are rooted in fear itself—our *own* fear actually. Sometimes we don't see it. Symptoms of fear—our tendency to compare ourselves to others, our feelings of insecurity and inadequacy, or our penchant for popularity, to name a few—are usually camouflaged and often subconscious. Our fears can even drive us to do the very things we despise.

It would be shortsighted to dismiss our problems as merely broken humanity, spiritual warfare, or simply the Fall.[24] The core of our faith, the essence of the gospel, is being compromised by our culture of fear and the industry that has emerged around it. Our deep-seated fear about the world, others, and ourselves is forging a version of church that is only a shadow of the real thing. As a result, an increasing number of Jesus followers and God seekers find themselves in a quandary about their faith. Many are disillusioned. Some are holding out for a better version to emerge. Others are giving up on faith altogether.

I am concerned that if we don't recover the essence of authentic church, if we don't repair the foundation of our faith that is being ravaged by fear, the prevailing culture could take our faith down and our lives along with it. A friend once told me that the opposite of faith is not doubt but fear. If my friend is right, then your faith and mine are only as strong as we are unafraid.

THE PARADOX OF ONE PERCENT

Our proclivity for fear says something about the quality of our faith. The people who should be most afraid often are not, and those who should be carefree are most afraid. Because I work globally, I learn from unlikely people in far-off places. Belinda and I lived in West Africa for six years and later returned to East Africa with our sons, then three and five years old. During those years and since, we've traveled fairly extensively, often to places with pressing needs because of disaster, disease, or war. Today I spend a fair bit of time moving between two populations: the world's most vulnerable, who are considered the bottom 1 percent by Western economic standards, and the very wealthy, or top 1 percent.[25] I spend my days connecting the top with the bottom, and vice versa, for this reason: they need each other. Both have something to give.

Some time ago while traveling through the Democratic Republic of Congo, a country devastated by years of war, a friend and I met a woman who described her experiences. She told us how her husband was killed in a cross fire between warring militias, how she was violently assaulted by soldiers who were supposed to protect her, and how she fled her village with her eight children under the cover of night. She forgave her perpetrators—"again and again," in her words—until she was healed. She started a small business and taught "her sisters" how to do the same. She also taught them how to forgive. Today she sings, she laughs, she keynotes at ceremonies in her community. When she walks into a room, she is honored with applause.

To the rest of the world, she is poor. By economic standards that may be so. Yet she is anything but poor. Our faith paled in comparison to hers; she towered in strength. We were afraid to cross the border into her country, yet she lives there, helping others flourish in one of the most difficult places in the world. We came to give, to pray, yet we found ourselves on our knees, asking her to pray for us.

I have often been surprised by the resilience, perseverance, and courage in places where I expected people to be riddled, even paralyzed, by fear. I have been equally surprised by the fear I find in people who are living comfortably, who have access to first-rate health care, top-tier education, and unbridled opportunity. Many are surprisingly afraid; some are even embarrassed by their chronic anxieties.[26] Research confirms this observation. In his essay "The Epidemic of Worry," David Brooks wrote, "According to World Health Organization, 18.2 percent of Americans report chronic anxiety while only 3.3 percent of Nigerians do."[27] People living near the bottom seem to fear less, while those living at the top fear more.

I find the same paradox revealed in different demographic groups in the United States. Ethnic faith communities—Hispanic, Congolese, Burmese, Arabic, to name only a few—as well as African American faith communities, often exhibit astounding faith in the face of immense challenges. Many on the margins economically, socially, or culturally overcome unjust treatment every day. They are excluded, scoffed at or jeered, overlooked, or simply forgotten, yet they bravely carry on. Still, years, even generations, of such treatment have left whole populations in our country feeling oppressed. Within these contexts uncommon faith is often forged, the kind of faith that is no longer afraid.

But isn't there an intuitive link between injustice, faith, and the absence of fear? Hard times forge strong faith. Strong faith, in turn, enables people to become less fearful. In short, suffering becomes the crucible in which resilient, genuine faith can be formed. Makes sense, right?

Maybe not. At least, not entirely.

Most people I know are experiencing suffering from one source or another—a wounded relationship, a physical malady, an impossible situation, an estranged child. But for many this formula simply doesn't work. They emerge from a season of suffering even more afraid than before. Anxiety is pervasive in our culture; the incidence of fear is on the rise.[28] Suffering doesn't automatically produce the kind of faith that overcomes fear.

On the whole the problems experienced by those who enjoy economic and social power do not seem to create the same depth of faith as do the kinds of suffering encountered in parts of Africa and Asia or on the refugee trail in the Middle East. The paradox of the 1 percent is an invitation to consider a hidden message that few have dared to explore. When we encounter the people whom Jesus called "the least of these," we generally shift into a charitable mode. Our response, we assume, is to offer help. Whether we choose to help or not, our posture is the same: giver to receiver, patron to client, or philanthropist to beneficiary. Such a posture isn't always bad. After all, God does call us to be generous. But when we shift into this mode of charity, we miss an important message that was central to the life and teaching of Jesus, a message that has the potential to rescue us from fear, overhaul our faith, and change our lives. Discovering that message and its implications—which is a major theme of this book—requires us first to make "the least of these" our teachers.

And surprising teachers they are.

WHAT THIS BOOK IS ABOUT

Break Open the Sky is about reclaiming our faith from a culture of fear so we can become emissaries of hope during portentous times. This book seeks to strip our faith to its most basic form, taking down its facade and dismantling its superstructure to gaze upon its pristine foundation, the piers of truth buried deep within the bedrock of God himself. *Break Open the Sky* is an invitation to dig beneath the superficial faith that has left us feeling adrift, anxious, or afraid so we can discover, or rediscover, the real thing. We owe it to God, and ourselves, to examine these essentials so we can turn our hopes into reality.

Break Open the Sky confronts simplistic, misleading notions that we've too easily believed. This book's central idea is that we have settled for a saccharine version of faith—a version of faith we must find the courage to question, confront, and dismantle in order to reconstruct our faith with an unwavering resolution to live it out. *Break Open the Sky* is an expedition into living a life of authentic faith, free from the fear that so often plagues our faith communities.

We can either turn away or choose to be brave.

This journey is not for the faint of heart.

Throughout these pages I search for a set of principles that form the bedrock of faith. My journey so far has surprised me, in part because what I've learned has come from unlikely places. I expected to learn from the eloquent, educated, or famous but instead have found wisdom among the least of these. In many cases my tutors have been the most vulnerable themselves, those who have suffered greatly while maintaining a holy, distinguishable, set-apart trust in God. In the process I've come to realize that much of what I had grown to depend upon was not essential to the Christian faith at all.

If you take this journey, I am convinced you will be surprised too.

While faith can, and should, shape culture, its essentials transcend it. God is absolute and relevant to all people for all time. If we believe a rediscovery of faith can correct the trajectory of disillusionment so many are experiencing, then the essence of faith will apply to all people regardless of geography, circumstances, or education. An entrepreneur from the Congo, a skater in Portland, and an aspiring attorney from Chicago will all have something in common if, in fact, they have tapped into these essentials.

We will explore three major themes. The first is *Truth*. We'll examine the central ideas in the life and teachings of Jesus, which are more relevant than ever for the post-truth culture in which we live, ideas that are usually tamed or diluted but which form the heart of faith and have the power to move us beyond fear. Second, we'll explore the power of *Love*, its revolutionizing character and liberating promise, why we so easily misunderstand its true nature and source, why faith is meaningless without it, and how it can become the foundation for a different way of living in a world increasingly bereft of love. Finally, we'll explore the notion of *Risk*, specifically how authentic faith and genuine love catapult us toward a life we've dreamed about but often don't have the guts to live. Along the way we will consider what it means to have a conversational relationship with God, a relationship free from the duty, drudgery, and fear that so often accompany the journey of faith.

Maybe you are disillusioned with faith or are struggling to close the gap between the promises of faith and what you experience day to day. Maybe you feel anxious or find yourself caving in to the fear around you. Perhaps you feel as if following Jesus has become so complicated and difficult that you are ready to give up. Or it's possible you've become so used to making decisions from a posture of fear that you are no longer aware of it. Sadly, fear can become a lens through which we see everything.

If so, I pray this book blows like a fresh wind through your soul.

One more thing before we set off on our journey together. For many years sociologists have predicted the decline of religion. Some have expected religion to die out altogether.[29] Instead, "a massive religious awakening is taking place around the world."[30] While church attendance is declining in the United States,[31] religion is not. Even the majority of those who self-identify as having no religious affiliation— "nones" as some people call them—"pray and believe in angels."[32] In short, those who predicted the end of religion were dead wrong.

So when the eminent philosopher Charles Taylor called our times a "Secular Age," some wondered if he had missed the mark. But for Taylor, secularization neither denied "the existence of God" nor affirmed "the triumph of science over religion." Instead it lowered ethical expectations, deemphasizing the essential goals of faith, goals that are impossible to fulfill apart from God. We must recognize that while religion is on the rise, it may not be the kind of religion that brings life.

To be sure, faith and religion can be two very different things. In recent years, said Matthew Rose commenting on Taylor, "life without God became imaginable," even as we claimed to be more religious than ever. Some even began to wonder "if Christian faith might be an obstacle to human well-being."[33] The humanist movement, for example, is gaining steam under the proviso that good is possible, maybe even better, without God.[34]

Admirably, Taylor was looking for a faith that would produce more than merely good Christian ethics or better "human flourishing."[35] Dallas Willard anticipated a similar crisis, calling for "men and women to be heroic in their faith and in spiritual character and power [because] the greatest danger to the Christian church today is that of pitching its message *too low.*"[36]

When the majority of Americans say they fear the wrath of God,[37] we can understand why church leaders want to make Christianity more palpable. But by presenting a more approachable God, have we pulled ourselves down rather than lifted others up? Have we reduced faith to mere self-help therapy and activism rather than faithfully representing the radical nature of the gospel with its promise and power to thoroughly overhaul human life and society so that onlookers cannot help but be drawn to God with wonder? By lowering the bar, have we lost our courage, our passion, our zeal for something greater, which in the end may be nothing more than the real thing—mere Christianity, as C. S. Lewis would say?

These questions haunt me; maybe they haunt you too. But my main interest is not to prove our faith is in jeopardy—the indicators are compelling enough for others to prove that. Instead I want to explore and pursue a different version of faith, one that is faithful to the person and nature of Jesus, one that transcends culture but is still deeply engaged with it, and one that is attractive to a dying world, not off-putting, proud, or smug.

In a very real sense, this book is nothing more than a quest for authentic faith in an age when authenticity is desperately needed. Dietrich Bonhoeffer said, "We can only achieve perfect liberty and enjoy fellowship with Jesus when . . . his call to absolute discipleship, is appreciated in its entirety." But appreciating the fullness of this call "is not a sort of spiritual shock treatment," Bonhoeffer explained. "Jesus asks nothing of us without giving us the strength to perform it. His commandment never seeks to destroy life, but to foster, strengthen and heal it."[38]

But we must pursue this call together, not alone, within the community of faith, as broken and disillusioned as we may be.

Someone recently asked me how I am able to remain hopeful in the face of so much fear and suffering. Our faith is indeed in crisis; the symptoms are daunting. But our God is greater than the problems we face. Like you, I grieve at the onset of another war or the latest coup d'état that drags another nation toward ruin. I get sick to my stomach when I hear stories of boys forced to fight in wars or girls sold into slavery. I weep at the infighting across much of our political, social, and religious landscape. Yet I also encounter extraordinary stories of hope—of churches living out versions of faith that truly distinguish them as lights on a hill,[39] of ordinary people fighting overwhelming odds to push back the effects of fear, racism, violence, oppression, or poverty. I meet people who choose to love despite having overwhelming reasons to become bitter.

Genuine change is hard work but within reach and entirely possible. Authentic faith is tangible. Love is near. Hope is real. We *can* break through to a new realm; our times demand an urgent response. Novelist Walter Mosley wrote:

> We are not trapped or locked up in these bones. No, no. We are
> free to change. And love changes us. And if we can love one
> another, we can break open the sky.[40]

Take this journey with me. Your risk now promises real change, not just for you, but for others as well. Our world, our culture, and our faith have reached a crisis point. We are living in a moment when we can choose to let our convictions slip away or we can double down on what is most important. Our faith is at stake. Our lives too.

Together, with God's help, we can break open the sky.

Part 1

TRUTH

The Spirit of God is the great unmasker of illusions,
the great destroyer of icons and idols. God's love for
us is so great that He does not permit us to harbor
false images, no matter how attached we are to
them. God strips those falsehoods from us no matter
how naked it may make us, because it is better to live
naked in truth than closed in fantasy.

—Brennan Manning

One

Truth Furiously Knocking

Better a cruel truth than a comfortable delusion.
—Edward Abbey

ormer Maryland poet laureate Lucille Clifton wrote a poem some years ago about the nature of truth. She finished her poem with a captivating line: "You might as well answer the door, my child, / the truth is furiously knocking."[1]

Last year the *Oxford Dictionary* chose *post-truth* as the word of the year, not because it was new—it's been around for more than a decade—but because Oxford recorded a significant spike in the word's usage. The *Oxford Dictionary* defines *post-truth* as "relating to or denoting circumstances in which objective facts are less influential in shaping public opinion than appeals to emotion and personal belief."[2] Both *post-truth* and *fake news,* a term used specifically to refer to "people who purposely fabricate stories for clicks and revenue,"[3] have become hotly debated topics.

Across all age groups in the United States, confidence in mass media has sunk to an all-time low. Only 32 percent of Americans say they trust the media is telling the truth, down 8 percentage points from last year.[4] When John Adams called facts "stubborn" in 1770, saying that "whatever may be our wishes, our inclinations, or the dictates of our passions, they cannot alter the state of facts and evidence,"[5] he may not have anticipated a day when facts would become mere decorations of opinion rather than germane to truth.

Truth is not what it used to be.

In the New Testament the Greek word for faith (*pistis*) essentially means "trust, confidence, assurance, and belief."[6] One of the capstone verses in all the Bible defines faith as "the substance of things hoped for, the evidence of things not seen."[7] Faith is belief, rooted in a commitment—a commitment anchored in substance, tangible evidence, in truth itself. And truth is anchored in fact. Jesus, who lived in time and space, actually referred to himself as "the way and *the truth* and the life."[8]

Faith without truth starts to crumble really fast. It's like having the proverbial rug pulled out from underneath or leaning against a paper wall. Faith without truth is scary.

And so it should be.

What if our growing unease about truth and the symptoms we feel, whether mere anxiety or full-on fear, is actually an invitation to take a hard look at our faith? What if our fear, whether corporate or personal, is really an opportunity to reason together, to consider the state of our faith, to reflect on its nature, to sift through its presuppositions and explore its implications? What if truth has been knocking for some time—maybe for years—but ever more furiously now in these urgent times?

If we are brave enough to take an honest look, we will find truth is insistent, not because it wants to harm or condemn. No, the nature of truth is to set free, to break open, to liberate.[9]

Several years ago the world was dramatically awakened to the deadly war in Syria when an image of the lifeless body of a three-year-old boy, Aylan Kurdi, surfaced in mainstream media. Still wearing his tiny shoes, blue shorts, and red T-shirt, Aylan washed up on a Turkish beach after a failed attempt to reach safety in Europe. Our hearts broke when we heard about Aylan's father, who tried to save his son.[10]

The image of Aylan became a tipping point in public opinion, drawing attention to a five-year-old war that had already claimed more than four hundred thousand civilian lives and forced more than eleven million Syrians to flee their homes. Regarding the image of Aylan, filmmaker Ken Burns observed that the "single image . . . [still] has that power to shock and arrest us."[11]

But within a few months, as the migration of hundreds of thousands of Syrian families pouring into Europe dominated news headlines, the possibility of refugees like Aylan and his family coming to the United States had stirred controversy and contention and even hostility.[12] The horrific terrorist attack in Paris on November 13, 2015, followed by the attack in San Bernardino, California, on December 2, 2015, led many to speculate that opening the door to refugees would lead to more terrorism, a fear further stoked by politicians and several candidates for the presidency in 2016.

The compassion sparked by Aylan's death was swept away by the prevailing winds of fear.

A day after the terrorist attack in San Bernardino, I addressed a group of people in nearby Santa Monica about the plight of Syrian refugees. Following a brief presentation, a gentleman who had visited Kenya and valued the role of faith in serving others asked me if I thought Islam was to blame for terrorism. I explained that, while I didn't agree with the tenets of Islam, I knew many Muslims who categorically rejected terrorism. He pressed me further. "But doesn't the Koran condone violence?" Carefully I said the same argument could be made about the Bible, especially the Old Testament. He pressed again, this time more stridently. His questions turned into comments, and he began to dominate the gathering. I realized he was more interested in making a point than in finding common ground.

As he continued to present his perspective, a woman near the back of the room with golden-gray hair and a smile like the midday sun raised her hand. "I meet Muslims all the time. We have great conversations. We talk about Jesus, and I often pray with them," she said. "I suppose I should be worried about getting my throat slit in the back of a taxi or something, but I am not. I am not afraid to die; I know where I am going. I choose to love."

All my theological explanations and data couldn't accomplish what this woman did by sharing her personal experience. With a few simple words, she shifted the tone of the room. Her story made me think of the apostle John's words: "This is how we know what love is: Jesus Christ laid down his life for us. And we ought to lay down our lives for our brothers and sisters."[13]

But how could two people, similar in many ways, arrive at such different conclusions? Both grieved the loss of life in San Bernardino the night before, and both cared passionately about the issues we were discussing. Both had a commitment to the Christian faith, even similar versions of that faith. Yet their perspectives couldn't have been more divergent. She chose to trust, while her counterpart chose to fear. She expressed love; he offered anger.

He sidestepped, dismissed, or shelved salient facts about refugees, Syria, and Islam, as well as certain essential truths about his faith, and allowed his inclinations and emotions to prevail. She allowed the substance of her faith, anchored in the historical life and message of Jesus, to help her overcome her fear, even as she recognized the brutal possibility of personal death.

His truth left him afraid while her truth helped her triumph over fear.

What Mr. Rogers and Jesus Had in Common

Fred Rogers, affectionately known as Mr. Rogers or even "Saint Fred" as of late,[14] hosted one of the longest-running shows in network television. He was awarded an honorary doctorate—his twenty-fifth—by Boston University some years ago. At the commencement ceremony Rogers was met with exuberant cheers from the student body as he invited them to sing along to the theme from his television program: "It's a beautiful day in the neighborhood. A beautiful day for a neighbor. Would you be mine?" All across the stadium people swayed to the rhythm of the well-known tune.[15] After the singing died down, the crowd now calm and attentive, Mr. Rogers said, "It's not the honors and the prizes and the fancy outsides of life which ultimately nourish our souls." Then he quoted *The Little Prince,* saying, *"L'essentiel est invisible pour les yeux:* what is essential is invisible to the eye."[16]

A man who dedicated his life to crafting visible stories at a time when image was becoming paramount, Mr. Rogers chose to point to unseen things as being essential. For Mr. Rogers the most important truth was hidden from sight. Or maybe he would say hidden in plain sight.

Jesus wasn't caught up in the fancy outside of life either. When he presented a series of eight principles or values, called the Beatitudes, at the outset of his Sermon on the Mount, he would have drawn a collective gasp from his audience. In just a few succinct statements, Jesus ran roughshod over the religious norms of his day by assigning virtue to a group of unlikely people: the poor, sad, meek, merciful, hungry, thirsty, peaceful, and persecuted.[17] Jesus conferred divine favor, or blessing, not on the revered moralists of his day, but on the ragtag outsiders. The respectable folk within earshot likely squirmed while the outcasts dropped their jaws and Jesus's disciples sat dumbfounded.

Jesus went on to make his case for fulfilling, not abolishing, the contemporary rules of faith, known in his day as "the Law," by putting into place something far better. He praised the doers, not the talkers, of the Law as "great in the kingdom of heaven" and punctuated his argument by saying anyone interested in this new version of faith must exceed the righteousness required by the Law.[18]

In these eight rather poetic statements, Jesus confronted what it meant to be blessed by God by redefining who is invited to live the good life. He sidestepped conventional wisdom, upending the notion that carefully minding a set of rules was God's intended path to virtue. Instead, Jesus spoke about a set of values so important and powerful they would not only fulfill the Law but exceed it altogether.

In the first century the rules of religious life were objective, taught regularly, and applied in minute detail. The Law was well known, and it permeated Jewish life. On the other hand, the values Jesus talked about would have been counterintuitive to the first-century mind, if not hidden altogether. At best, they would have seemed paradoxical and, at worst, completely foreign to the contemporary concept of the righteous life. In the first century a person's predicament—such as blindness, illness, or poverty—was a sign of disfavor by God, sometimes even thought to indicate a curse. How could poverty, grief, hunger, or thirst be associated with blessing or divine acceptance? How could the poor, meek, mournful, and merciful be happy or blessed?

Jesus no doubt offended, confused, and sparked disbelief in many. But he pointed to something important, something essential and life changing. With these provocative words Jesus unveiled a powerful truth: what we often consider most important in life is, in fact, not, and conversely, what we sometimes laugh at, look down upon, or outright dismiss might be, in fact, essential. For Jesus, like Mr. Rogers, the most important things in life are invisible. Only those willing to shut their eyes would see.

The idea that truth is hidden is a recurrent theme in the Bible. When Nicodemus, a prestigious religious leader, sought out Jesus one night to offer some modest flattery and ask a few questions, Jesus told Nicodemus he couldn't "see his kingdom" unless he was "born again." Nicodemus was offended:

"How can this be?" Nicodemus asked.

"You are Israel's teacher," said Jesus, "and do you not understand these things? . . . I have spoken to you of earthly things and you do not believe; how then will you believe if I speak of heavenly things?"[19]

In contrast to "seeing the kingdom," seeing through the world's eyes, said George Weigel, "is to see things in a distorted way. Original sin, we may say, was the original astigmatism . . . [distorting] our perception of the human person and the human condition." The incarnation, where God enters our human story in the form of a vulnerable baby, begins a sort of "vision correction through inversion," according to Weigel, "a pattern that continues through the gospels":

> Jesus doesn't evangelize the principalities and powers (although
> they, too, are welcome to listen and learn); he goes to the
> outcasts, including the lepers and prostitutes, to announce and
> embody a kingdom in which Israel's king is not just [king] of
> the people of Israel but the whole world.[20]

Earlier in the gospel of John, the apostle says regarding Jesus that even "though the world was made through him, the world did not recognize him."[21] Important truth, indispensable truth, truth that matters comes by *revelation*, "the divine or supernatural disclosure to humans."[22] Without revelation, it seems, we are prone to rejecting truth. More often than not, we simply cannot see it, and what we do see is distorted. What may be apparent to us, what is seemingly intuitive, may actually be false. While what we may dismiss because we consider it foolish or irrelevant may actually be the essential truth we are missing.

It seems Fred Rogers was echoing Jesus when quoting *The Little Prince*. Truth is hard to find, even when it is staring us in the face. "The blind will see and those who see will become blind," said Jesus.[23]

We need God's help to know what is true and what isn't. Our faith depends on it.

WHY IT'S CALLED THE GOSPEL

Many would consider the Beatitudes to be basic to the life and teaching of Jesus. Yet they remain controversial today. Dallas Willard, for example, insists they are merely announcements about who is invited to participate in the good life.[24] The poor, the hungry, the sad, the left-out are invited to experience God's favor, perhaps for the first time in history. Certainly Jesus did champion the marginalized and introduced what he called a kingdom, a way of life that was very different from the conventional thinking of his day. But Willard cautions against reading the Beatitudes as a new set of virtues, or ethics, to live by. "The poor in spirit are blessed as a result of the kingdom of God being available to them," wrote Willard, not because spiritual poverty is a virtuous or "praiseworthy condition."[25] Willard quoted Alfred Edersheim to drive home his point:

> Jesus did not say, "Blessed are the poor in spirit because they
> are poor in spirit." He did not think, "What a fine thing it is to
> be destitute of every spiritual attainment or quality. It makes
> people worthy of the kingdom." And we steal away the much
> more profound meaning of his teaching about the availability
> of the kingdom by replacing the state of spiritual impoverish-
> ment—in no way good in itself—with some supposedly
> praiseworthy state of mind or attitude that "qualifies" us for
> the kingdom.[26]

Poverty, whether physical or spiritual, does not qualify anyone for divine favor. Jesus is announcing something powerful, something altogether different, something much better than the rules of his day. His listeners would have been shocked.

But Willard's logic breaks down with the latter Beatitudes. Jesus may very well be announcing the availability of divine favor to the poor, powerless, sad, hungry, and thirsty in the first four statements, but when he shifts to the pure in heart, the merciful, the peacemakers, and the persecuted, he is doing more than announcing an invitation. He is commending those who are living out a set of "kingdom" values. Willard's interpretation of the Beatitudes is important, but it's incomplete.

Eugene Peterson and other well-respected theologians[27] present the Beatitudes as a distilled set of principles or, better, values that summarize what Jesus referred to as God's "kingdom," meaning what it looks like when God's "will [is] done, on earth as it is in heaven."[28] These values were, and are, so radically different from what we assume to be God's will that they seem impossible to live out. Within this impossibility lies a mystery, however—a surprise so radical that it became known as the gospel, or "good news." In these Beatitudes, Jesus both announced this breakthrough news and conferred it upon the least likely recipients.

There is a logic inherent in his invitation. If God is making his favor available for even the least of these, then everyone else is included too. This radical grace was—and is—available for all people bold enough to pursue his outrageous offer.

Bringing together Willard's and Peterson's views of the Beatitudes results in a more complete picture. While we recognize that only God can empower such a radical way of life, the Beatitudes represent both an announcement of the purpose of God to bless all people and a description of that blessed life through a set of kingdom values. Jesus was in effect inviting us into a new way to live, akin to Weigel's "inversion," through an upside-down set of priorities. It's a way of life that only God can make possible for us and establish in the world. These kingdom values cannot be earned or awarded based on merit, as those who have tried this radical lifestyle on their own have discovered. But for *anyone* willing to take up the invitation, there are profound lessons to be learned from the people who have been left out of God's favor for so long. By showcasing the least of these, God invites all of us to encounter, experience, and live out his divine favor.

The implications of the Sermon on the Mount were far-reaching. The sermon showed that those who thought they were living the good life, a life blessed by God, were, in fact, not. And those who were on the outside looking in — the outcasts, the down-and-out, the ragamuffins — were closer to God than they ever dreamed.

Two thousand years later we find ourselves in exactly the same place. Many people are living anxious lives. The demands of career, school, and family are taxing, if not overwhelming. The psychological stress occasioned by vagaries in the economy, the vitriol of our political discourse, or the threat of global terrorism leaves us feeling edgy and ragged. We feel anxiety but may not even know what makes us afraid.

And then there are the conversations we have with ourselves. Most people measure themselves against someone or something and then fight their inner doubts to believe they, too, have what it takes to do something meaningful with their lives. This inner tension creates a longing for some shard of shalom, some personal peace, some measure of rest. So we scurry to our faith communities in search of well-being, only to find the same pecking order, the same penchant for success, the same proclivity for performance from which we sought shelter.

Into this milieu Jesus introduces eight poster children: the poor, the mourners, the meek, the hungry and thirsty, the merciful, the pure in heart, the peacemakers, and the persecuted. Interestingly, they were featured prominently throughout the Old Testament and would have been referred to as *anawim,* literally "bowed down," in Jesus's day.[29] Mary, Jesus's mother, would have been described as anawim and maybe also Jesus himself. Anawim were known as the pious poor—humble, meek, hungry, and thirsty but also God-fearing. Several years ago I worshipped in a church in DC that, according to the pastor, serves both "the members of Congress and those that clean their offices." The pastor prayed powerfully for the anawim in the city, that we might see them, love them, and include them in our midst. It is these anawim who are the blessed, even happy, poster children in the Great Sermon. According to Jesus, the very people we may be tempted to pity, look down on, or dismiss are actually the choice subjects for introducing, explaining, and exhibiting the kingdom of God.

The idea seems as preposterous now as it must have seemed in Jesus's day.

Incidentally, to the poster children this news was good, outrageously good. No wonder they called it the gospel. But to the rest of the crowd, including perhaps some of Jesus's disciples, this news was blasphemous, ridiculous, and personally threatening. Jesus was dismantling all they knew about faith, the way in which they viewed God, and their idea of what it was to have divine favor. Jesus's disciples and anyone else listening would have seriously questioned his mental well-being.

Why did Jesus create the controversy? Was he bent on offending? Was he prone to inflammatory words? Or did he offend his listeners so they would consider taking up his invitation to what Willard called the "with-God life"[30]?

TWO ROADS DIVERGED

Jesus had his reasons for offering the provocative truths of the Beatitudes, and they are surprising. For Jesus, "cruel truth," the idea that truth must sometimes offend in order to awaken, was preferable to "comfortable delusion."

Yet before tackling the question of why Jesus made these statements, let's first consider their implications. Imagine two groups of people traveling on different roads. Both roads diverged from a fork, so far in the distance that the people can no longer see it in the rearview mirror. For the moment let's set aside the questions of how the people ended up on one road or the other or how many other groups were also traveling. On one road are people who are trying hard to be good, meaning that they work hard at being kind, going to church, doing well in school and work or raising children. Though they don't like office gossip, they can't help but get caught up in it once in a while. They keep in touch with friends on social media, give to charity, donate a few hours here and there to a local food bank, and work hard to stay in shape. And they stand ready to help any of the people on the second road who might be in need.

The second road is filled with people who, for the most part, appear to be unlucky. Many of them are unemployed. Some are grieving the death of a loved one. Others are fleeing a country torn by war or that offers little freedom or opportunity. Though they try, some simply cannot seem to make their mortgage payments. A few on this road seem oddly out of touch with reality. They are inordinately concerned with the needs of those around them, pray more than normal—albeit in an unrefined manner—and focus undue attention on obscure parts of the world where injustice seems to be the norm. Occasionally they are the butt of jokes made by the people on the other road.

As you observe passersby on both roads, you notice the people on the second road seem to be more carefree than those on the first. Those in the first group are consumed with their goal: they want to finish their journey. They are focused, driven, even obsessive, insisting that nothing will prevent them from completing their mission. They are doing good in the world, to the best of their ability, and they know they will be rewarded for it.

Those in the second group seem to laugh more often despite their unlucky predicaments. Some even help each other along the way and are not afraid to slow down so others can catch up. Their ideas seem idealistic and impracticable, and their passion for their cause can be off-putting. They always seem a bit surprised when good things happen to them and consider themselves lucky.

If you recognize yourself on one of these roads and are starting to feel bad about your life, hang in there. I've spent most of my life on the first road and still drift into its lanes more often than I'd like to admit. When I do, I experience anxiety, boredom, frustration, and, indeed, fear. For me, these emotions serve as warning lights. They tell me I am in the wrong lane or on the wrong road and remind me to change course. God's mercy often comes disguised.

Now a question: Remember the man and woman from Santa Monica? One inclined to fear and one committed to love? On which road does each travel?

And another more salient question: On which road do you travel?

Could it be that the message of Jesus has been so muted through the ages that it has left many of us bereft of the joy, peace, and blessing we set out to find? When we look around—whether across the church pew, to the adjacent cubicle, or at the neighbor down the street—we see family, friends, and acquaintances with whom we are prone to compare ourselves and compete without realizing what we are doing. Sometimes we experience a fear so pervasive that it saturates our thoughts and emotions without our recognizing it. We may talk about bravery or risk, but we are more likely to capitulate to the fear around us than to confront it.

Thankfully the two roads are not far apart. It's never too late to veer toward the other. Jesus constantly offers an invitation to change, always waits, and even provides the means to do it. God likes hard left (or right) turns, and he loves on- and off-ramps.

Cruel truth, in the end, is merciful. But it requires courage to take a hard, honest look at ourselves.

CASE IN POINT

Let's meet one of the anawim Jesus was talking about in his Sermon on the Mount.

A handful of years ago in a certain country in Africa, a friend of mine whom we'll call Vincent was suddenly and unjustly thrown in prison. One of his colleagues had falsely accused him of rolling his eyes when a war survivor was telling her story on the local radio station. Vincent was imprisoned because someone said he was thinking derogatory thoughts about members of another tribe, even though there was no evidence to support the claim.

A few days later my colleague and I visited Vincent's wife—whom we'll call Chantel—and their four children. They lived in a simple house consisting of three small rooms with marred concrete floors, a table made from unfinished planks, two benches, and a propane cooking stove. Most days Chantel farmed a small plot of land near their house, growing bananas to help make ends meet. It was evening when we met, and she was finished with her work. We talked about Chantel's husband—the rhythms of prison life, who was planning to take food to him, and how often she could visit. She understood the gravity of the situation. She knew others who had been imprisoned without charges for months, even years. Some never returned home.

After we talked awhile, Chantel gathered her children, all under the age of seven, and asked if we could pray. A lone candle lit the room as we stood together holding hands, all seven of us. We prayed and then sang "Amazing Grace" in two languages. We told her we would do everything possible to get her husband released. She told us she would keep praying. We promised to pray too.

As we walked away from her house under the moonlit sky, I couldn't help but reflect on the sharp difference between Chantel's disposition and mine. I was angered by the injustice and frustrated that my request to government officials was met with silence, despite my having some cachet due to my position. My perceived influence was inadequate to bring about a resolution. I felt helpless.

Chantel felt helpless too, but she was unshaken—her faith tangible, her disposition peaceful.

I asked myself if I would trade all the things I'd learned for a faith that doesn't buckle during a crisis, that endures under strain, that isn't fundamentally fearful. In the thick of her trial, she exuded strength, so much so that her four kids looked to her for assurance, for hope. She could not guarantee that their father would come home; she knew too much about her country to make such a promise. She also knew that there was no fallback plan. She had no college degree, no savings account to lean on. Still, she rose to pray, vulnerable yet dignified, stricken but unmoved, her voice strong, her countenance resolute, her faith unwavering.

I am convinced genuine faith is more accessible than we imagine. If we were to shed our goals, programs, plans, products, and all the bells and whistles that have become ubiquitous in the Western church, what would remain? What if we were to pursue a simpler faith, a faith with more spiritual substance and less dependency on external markers, a faith with more freedom, more deference, and more trust but not as easy to objectively measure. Perhaps that would be a faith capable of inspiring confidence in what we hope for and evidence of what we cannot see,[31] a faith strong enough to enable a woman who just lost her husband and the father of her children to sing songs of courage to weary souls.

I wonder if that version of faith is what Jesus spoke of in his famous sermon.

Sometimes we have to close our eyes so we can see. Fred Rogers lived that way; some people dismissed him. Now he's "Saint Fred." Why? Because he lived like the people Jesus called blessed. Fred Rogers didn't have to live that way; he chose to. He could have lived as though he deserved something for his achievement, but he didn't.

Jesus inaugurated something revolutionary back then and still offers it today. He presents a radically new and disconcerting version of faith, not to offend, but to jolt us sufficiently so that we will reconsider— radically reconsider—what is most important in life and how to live that out. Jesus's version of faith doesn't come naturally. It is hard won, but not by pulling ourselves up by our bootstraps, self-help style. It is a gift, but accepting it requires courage. It is available to those brave enough to accept God's invitation to take and eat with the confidence that he will neither slap their hands nor send them the bill.

Truth often stings before it liberates and brings healing. We typically don't associate truth with overcoming anxieties or fear, yet truth is often the place to begin. We must take an honest look in the mirror with the full confidence that God will not condemn us but rather will invite us into a whole new way to live, free from fear and with the capacity to genuinely love. After all, Jesus didn't come "into the world to condemn the world, but in order that the world might be saved through him."[32]

To understand how radically different Jesus's teaching on faith was—and still is—we must reconsider an essential truth in the life of faith, a truth so central that all others hang upon it. Too often our faith is laden with myriad strength-sapping bolt-ons, leaving us to ask if that is all there is. When we recover the essence of the gospel, free from the dos and don'ts that so often accompany religion, we cannot help but feel emancipated. In its raw, original form, the truth we encounter in the next chapter is indispensable, a bedrock idea upon which our faith is built.

Two

A Banana Peel for the Orthodox Foot

We are suspicious of grace.
We are afraid of the very lavishness
of the gift.

—Madeleine L'Engle

I n the opening scene of *Happy,* a documentary that explores the nature of happiness, we meet Manoj Singh, a rickshaw driver from India.[1] He lives with his wife and three children in a one-room home constructed of rusted corrugated metal held together with plastic tarps. When asked about his life, he said, "I am not poor, but I am the richest person." He proudly talks about his work as a rickshaw driver in the crowded streets, dismissing the monsoons, sweltering heat, and occasional abuse from drunk passengers as mere inconveniences. He said his home is "good" even though it doesn't protect his family from the monsoons. Sometimes they can afford only rice with a bit of salt. "But we are still happy," he said.

Stunning. How could Manoj say he is happy when, from our perspective, the most basic elements of happiness are absent? Manoj and his family function near the bottom caste in a country that claims it has graduated from such a system. They are eking out a living amid grinding poverty. Their home is ramshackle, exposed, without title or deed. There is no running water or sanitation to speak of. Manoj's kids have little chance for quality education. Any disruption—drought, illness, economic downturn—could sabotage their very chance of survival.

But somehow in the midst of all this, Manoj is happy.

If Jesus were to give his Great Sermon today, he might stand atop the garbage heap in Kolkata and proclaim Manoj "blessed." Afterward Jesus might visit the Singh home and share a meal with the family. He might propose a toast to their friendship, tell them about his plans for the world—along with his plans for Manoj and his family—and might even ask for their help. He would undoubtedly make Manoj's children laugh and pray a divine blessing over them before he left. Manoj and his family would likely remember their evening as the day God smiled with favor upon them.

MANOJ VS. MASLOW

If people like Manoj can be happy, does that mean we should all seek poverty? This question leads to another, more fundamental, question, one that has been asked since the dawn of time: What makes people happy?

The dominant theory that has shaped modern thought about happiness is Abraham Maslow's hierarchy of needs, which has been routinely taught in introductory psychology courses since shortly after it was defined in 1954. According to Maslow's hierarchy, physical needs, such as food and safety, must be met before other, more lofty desires, such as love, respect, and what he calls self-actualization, can be realized.[2] But Manoj would disagree, maybe adamantly.

Interestingly, research supports Manoj, not Maslow.

Gallup conducted a survey on concepts related to well-being around the world. Over sixty thousand participants from 123 countries participated in the study between 2005 and 2010. Each participant answered questions regarding six aspects of life, patterned after the categories in Maslow's model: basic needs, safety, social needs, respect, mastery, and autonomy. The respondents also "rated their well-being across three discrete measures: life evaluation (a person's view of his or her life as a whole), positive feelings (day-to-day instances of joy or pleasure), and negative feelings (everyday experiences of sorrow, anger, or stress)." The results were surprising. According to Ed Diener, a psychologist at the University of Illinois, "Although the most basic needs might get the most attention when you don't have them, you don't need to fulfill them in order to get benefits" from other, loftier needs. "Even when we are hungry, for instance, we can be happy with our friends."[3]

The Gallup data challenged decades of conventional thought. Maslow's theory led social scientists to prioritize immediate needs over the social and spiritual aspects of human life. Economic well-being was thought to be the primary predicator for happiness. But Maslow was wrong. It turns out people can be happy even when their basic needs are unfulfilled. Wealth and health don't necessarily bring happiness. In fact, people like Manoj will often deprive themselves of basic needs to save some small bit of money for future dreams, boldly leaping over steps in Maslow's hierarchy.[4] Conversely, when basic needs are fulfilled or exceeded and even social needs are satisfied, people aren't necessarily self-actualized.

Maslow's hierarchy has begun to unravel.

Even policy-making institutions, including the United Nations, are redefining the concept of well-being. A UN resolution identified happiness as a "fundamental human goal." The resolution noted that the GDP indicator does not "adequately reflect the happiness and well-being of people."[5] The "World Happiness Report," which ranks countries according to a happiness index based on factors including life expectancy, social support, freedom to make life choices, government corruption, and the practice of generosity, showed intriguing results.[6] While Western nations dominate the top ten, there are some surprising countries listed in the top fifty, including Nicaragua and Uzbekistan, which are featured on the most-improved list in 2016.[7] Nigeria, where the average annual income is only three hundred dollars, has traditionally ranked high, even though it slipped in 2016.

Equally surprising is the list of countries becoming less happy. In the United States, where the baby-boomer generation is still considered the wealthiest generation in US history, the suicide rate has surged to a thirty-year high,[8] and antidepressants are the most prescribed drug of choice, with nearly 120 million prescriptions per year.[9] In the land where dreams are made, happiness is slipping. Still, a stunning 81 percent of eighteen- to twenty-five-year-olds said that getting rich was their most important goal in life.[10] Fame and beauty also rank high as perceived sources of happiness, even though celebrities are four times more likely to commit suicide than members of the general public.[11]

Interestingly, one study claims wealth and health have little impact on happiness but genetics do. The so-called FAAH gene makes the protein that yields feelings of pleasure and pain. People with a certain version of FAAH tend to be happier, according to new research cited by the *Guardian*.[12] Perhaps that's not surprising after all. Most of us can name someone we might call sanguine, buoyant, or just cheerful who seems happier, on average, than others.

Happiness, it seems, is not as easily pigeonholed as we'd thought. If wealth and health cannot produce it and genes are arbitrary, what reliably predicts happiness?

THE ELEGANT ANSWER

Not long ago some former colleagues of mine organized a group of people to welcome a Somali family at the airport in Minneapolis. You may be familiar with the refugee program in the United States that legally resettles families from countries where they have experienced religious or political persecution. Often the families fled their homes due to war or violence. Many have lost family members. Most have been waiting in refugee camps for years, sometimes decades. Still the world's poster child for failed states, Somalia is home to warring factions, terrorism, and piracy. The people of Somalia have suffered greatly.

But at the Minneapolis–St. Paul International Airport, a different story was being written. A group of volunteers from a local church welcomed a Somali family with three banners displaying the word "WELCOME" in large block letters—one banner in English, a second in Arabic, and a third in Somali. Utterly surprised, the family asked, "Which diplomat was flying on our plane with us?" They were speechless when a colleague explained that the warm welcome, expressed in the large colorful banners, was actually for them. They were the esteemed guests, the VIPs, not anyone else.

After they gathered themselves from their shock, with tears in their eyes, the Somali family members whispered, "We have never . . . been . . . welcomed . . . ever . . . in our lives."

When Jesus proclaimed favor upon the most unlikely people in the first century, their response would probably have been just the same as our Somali friends' reaction. They would no doubt have been speechless. Why? Because no one had ever welcomed them before either.

Dallas Willard paraphrases the opening line of the Sermon on the Mount this way:

Blessed are the spiritual zeros — the spiritually bankrupt, deprived and deficient, the spiritual beggars, those without a wisp of "religion" — when the kingdom of the heavens comes upon them.[13]

The people upon whom Jesus conferred blessing were the beat-up, overlooked, unwanted, taken-for-granted people of the world, the ones most consider failures, losers, bottom dwellers. As Willard suggests, these are the folks who "really can't make heads nor tails of religion."[14] They don't consider themselves worthy of a shred of divine favor. Even in their wildest dreams, they wouldn't entertain such an idea.

On the other hand, those in the crowd listening to Jesus who were of significant pedigree or who kept the Law scrupulously, especially the priests and teachers of the Law, would have considered themselves natural recipients of divine favor.

The nature of the human heart is to gravitate toward rules—no matter how arbitrary or trivial—as a standard for determining righteousness. Those who don't comply are left out, held back, or pushed down. So when Jesus pointed to a set of people who didn't qualify according to the standards of the day and said they were recipients of divine favor, he showed the crowd that rule keeping is not what matters most.

Theologians have often portrayed spiritual poverty as "something good in its own right and thus deserving of blessing," even though poverty, in a natural sense, is almost always considered an evil to overcome. But Dallas Willard turned this sort of thinking on its head. "Jesus did not say, 'Blessed are the poor in spirit *because* they are poor in spirit,'" wrote Willard. "He did not think, 'What a fine thing it is to be destitute of every spiritual attainment or quality.'" Rather, the "poor in spirit are called 'blessed' by Jesus, not because they are in a meritorious condition, but because, *precisely in spite of and in the midst of their ever so deplorable condition,* the rule of the heavens has moved redemptively upon and through them by the grace of Christ."[15]

By conferring blessing upon those widely thought to be undeserving, Jesus put into motion an idea so revolutionary that today we are still seeking to understand it. He showed us that the reason for divine favor is not us but solely him. The God of the universe doesn't award his favor, his blessing, his love according to our merit. We do not gain blessing by fulfilling the rules of the day—even the moral ones—or because of some talent we possess or accomplishment we have achieved, no matter how impressive. The apostle Paul put it plainly: "For it is by grace you have been saved, through faith—and this is not from yourselves, it is the gift of God—not by works, so that no one can boast."[16]

These words of Paul are widely known and often quoted in the church today. Since the Reformation the words *sola gratia,* by "grace alone," have been a mantra for many Christian traditions. We preach grace, pray it, and talk about it all the time. Yet for all our thinking and talking about grace, it remains a rare commodity in our day-to-day lives. Why is that? Why does our way of life betray our beliefs on this point? Too often criticism, judgment, unforgiveness, and gossip plague our experience, leaving many would-be Christians disillusioned. Many come to dismiss the promises of the Christian community as empty talk. We encounter people who have been offended or wounded by their experience within the faith community. Just yesterday a friend asked me why his community was so short on offering grace.

This phenomenon is not limited to a few pockets of the church, nor is it a fleeting occurrence. Social trust is eroding at a record pace within the Christian community as well as in the society at large. Only 19 percent of millennials agree that "people can be trusted," compared to 31 percent of generation X and 40 percent of baby boomers.[17] Social pecking orders, whether explicit or unstated, are so pervasive that many of us don't realize that we are constantly being sized up according to some, often hidden, standard. This ubiquitous social comparison reinforces the already vicious spiral of attempting to do more and be better in order to be accepted, which fuels the fear and anxiety that we are not good enough. The very idea of community is withering as a result: "We're living in a dissolving age," where the dominant threat is "untethered individualism," wrote R. R. Reno, editor of *First Things.*[18]

Could it be that the idea of undeserved favor is still novel, still unfamiliar, still revolutionary? If this is indeed the sine qua non of faith,[19] an essential truth and the cornerstone of our relationship with our Creator and with one another, why is it so hard to wrap our minds around the very possibility? Just like our Somali friends, we cannot fathom such an audacious gift. The keystone of faith—and the source of our happiness—remains elusive despite its simplicity, elegance, and availability. Grace is still the hardest thing for us to embrace.

But why?

NONRECIPROCAL

Some years ago, about midway through our first stint in Africa, Belinda and I were invited to the home of friends who lived near the gorgeous city of Toulouse in southern France. We met through mutual friends when the medical ship that was our home briefly stopped in the port city of Bordeaux to refuel before sailing on to West Africa. Belinda and I were leading Mercy Ships' training programs then and were looking for a venue to debrief three teams who would soon be returning from several months of service in Africa. Our French friends insisted we debrief our group of thirty-five people at their home. They also insisted we come a day or two early to enjoy the French countryside. On the heels of an intense season of preparing to return to Africa, we thought the idea of spending a few days away from the sound of ship generators and the constant smell of diesel oil sounded delightful. We gladly accepted their invitation.

When we drove up the long, winding road to their house, we realized we had misunderstood what they meant by the word *house*. We later learned that the French word for house (*maison*) can mean a lot of different things. In this case it meant a fifty-room chateau set in a verdant valley amid rolling hills blanketed with vineyards as far as the eye could see. We were stunned. After exchanging greetings and receiving an introduction to their chateau, our new friends ushered us into a dining room with twenty-foot ceilings, marble floors, and an array of glorious impressionist paintings. A massive fireplace with flaming logs dominated the far wall. Before us stood a table adorned with silver cutlery, finely glazed dishes, fresh baguettes, and a bottle of red wine.

"Now we must go," our hosts explained in broken English. "The food is in the kitchen. *Bon appétit!*"

We did our best to camouflage our shock with effusive thank-yous, delivered between the customary four kisses. We waved as they drove away in their vintage Mercedes. Then we closed the door in silence and locked eyes, our jaws dropping in disbelief. After living for nearly three years in a ten-by-ten-foot cabin aboard a hospital ship crammed with 350 of our closest friends, here we were in southern France, alone in a mansion, a bottle of wine from their private vintage on the table, a fire blazing before us, and French cuisine on the stove.

Tears welled up in Belinda's eyes.

I wish I could say that my immediate response was overwhelming joy or happiness or even gratitude, but it wasn't. Instead, I was overcome by a single thought: *What have we done to deserve this?* We had met this French couple only a few hours earlier. We knew nothing of their lives or their story, let alone their wealth. We hadn't served them. We hadn't impressed them. They owed us nothing. How could they be so kind? How could they trust us with so much?

After working through my consternation, my next emotion was guilt. I immediately tried to compensate by offering ideas for how we could tangibly thank our hosts—things we could do, connections we could make, stories we could tell. But we knew there was nothing we could do to repay their lavish kindness. Anything we tried to do would be a paltry attempt to accommodate our needs, not theirs. It might even offend them.

Finally letting go of our guilt, we relinquished our almost overwhelming desire to reciprocate in some way. We took a deep breath, poured a glass of wine, and enjoyed our extravagant evening.

That day remains one of the most memorable of our lives.

It's funny how the human heart feels it must return every favor, no matter how extraordinary or out of reach.

By now you see the connection. Accepting that we are loved for no other reason than the God of the universe loves us—it's in his very being and nature to do so—is the hardest thing you and I will ever do.

Grace is nonreciprocal.

Maybe we struggle to believe in grace because we are trapped in a world that defines itself by scarcity. Raj Raghunathan, author of *If You're So Smart, Why Aren't You Happy?* says the missing ingredient in our sense of well-being is an abundance mind-set. In many arenas—at school, on the athletic field, on the stage, in the office—our lives are defined by a scarcity mind-set. Everything seems to be in limited supply, and we are accustomed to a winner-take-all result. We cannot fathom a world in which everyone could win. In a recent interview Raghunathan said:

> One extreme is a kind of scarcity-minded approach, that my win is going to come at somebody else's loss, which makes you engage in social comparisons. And the other view is what I would call a more abundance-oriented approach, that there's room for everybody to grow.[20]

In certain creative fields, such as software development and advertising, people perform better if they adopt an abundance mind-set because they focus on the process of producing something great rather than win/lose outcomes.

It seems to me that an abundance mind-set is a close cousin to grace.

GOD MUST BE CRAZY

One reason it may be hard to accept unmerited favor or pursue an abundance mind-set is that we so desperately want to be good, to offer some shred of merit, something worthwhile, something earned. Unconsciously, we try to assuage our guilt and fear and preserve our dignity by proving our ability to fix our broken condition. In his book *Between Noon and Three: Romance, Law, and the Outrage of Grace,* Robert Farrar Capon captures the human response to grace in striking language:

> Restore to us, Preacher, the comfort of merit and demerit. Prove
> for us that there is at least something we can do, that we are still,
> at whatever dim recess of our nature, the masters of our relation-
> ships. . . . But do not preach us grace. . . . We insist on being
> reckoned with. Give us something, anything; but spare us the
> indignity of this indiscriminate acceptance.[21]

When we join with our brothers and sisters whom the world calls the least of these by admitting that we have nothing to give but everything to gain, we unleash a torrent of grace. It floods our souls with supernatural strength. It cleanses our minds with hope. It purifies our words and actions so thoroughly that we are finally able to truly love, offering to others an unanxious presence, an uncommon kindness, a subtle joy. The French have a saying, *L'amour de Dieu est folie,* which means the "love of God is folly," due to its incomprehensible nature.

Maybe God is more crazy than we think.

In one of his parables, Jesus presents a manager who pays the same wage to the workers who show up an hour before quitting time as to those who worked all day.[22] In another he celebrates a son who has wasted his father's inheritance and compromised the family name while his brother has kept all the rules.[23] Brennan Manning calls this grace so amazing that it "offends" even to the point of vulgarity.[24] Not surprisingly, this wild grace becomes a roadblock for the person seeking to earn spiritual significance. Yet it's upon this cornerstone truth, this central axiom, where the blessing of God is entirely unmerited and true happiness is built.

HOW TO BE HAPPY

Deyon Stephens is the cofounder of Mercy Ships. She and her husband, Don, are tremendous people, leaders, and friends. Years ago someone told Deyon that she deserved some time away. In response Deyon said something I've never forgotten. "Actually, I don't deserve anything," she said. "I deserve death. Everything else is grace."

What if we all lived as if we didn't deserve anything good—ever? How different would the world be if we saw every good thing in life as a gift of God's grace? Would we be more inclined to give grace to others? Would we hold on to things less tightly—our stuff, our expectations, even our reputations? Would we honor more, encourage more, love more, and even lavish more on others?

That sounds a lot like poverty of spirit, doesn't it?

And what if this humility were to pave the way for a spirit of abundance, whereby we would freely lavish grace on one another? Would such a disposition free us from the ugliness of comparison, competition, and insecurity—the manifestations of fear? Would we be less afraid?

And fearing less, would we then create more room for grace—both for ourselves and for others—thereby having a greater capacity to both receive and give love?

And having a greater capacity for love, would we find ourselves happier?

Happiness is not a state that is earned. It is a response, usually automatic, to undeserved grace. And underserved grace reveals something salient about God: his nature. God gives grace because he loves. When we give grace, we love too.

When Jesus lifted up the poor, meek, merciful, thirsty, and persecuted as poster children for blessing, he wasn't saying that we should seek poverty, sadness, or persecution in order to curry favor with him. No, he was inviting us into a way of life in which grace, favor, blessing, and love are lavished upon the kind of people who don't lay claim to them, who know in every fiber of their being that they cannot earn those things. For such folk, who know from the bottom of their souls to the last neuron in their brains that they do not deserve grace, their only response can be joy.

"Happy are those who . . ."[25]

The life of authentic faith can begin only with grace—vulgar grace, the kind that offends before it's welcomed. All other versions of faith will topple over or fade away, like the house built on sand that Jesus talked about. Self-righteousness, self-effort, and even self-actualization are all beds of sand. The only unequivocal foundation of faith is grace.

Unfortunately, we often give lip service to grace but continue to live by the pecking order of comparison and entitlement. How can we really live differently? *First, let go of any entitlements.* I realize in a world where we constantly talk about human rights, the idea of letting go of what we may feel we're entitled to is counterintuitive, even countercultural. Someone said, "Never seek justice for yourself, but never cease to give it." Relinquishing your claims, your rights, your attachments unleashes a deluge of grace that will set you apart, strikingly apart, so much so that people will ask how you got that way.

Second, accept that you are accepted. This is the hardest thing you'll ever do. To fully accept that you are unconditionally loved is a lifelong pursuit. This is the central truth of the universe, the idea behind creation, the supreme motive in the heart of God, and the reason angels sing and dance. To the degree you can comprehend this truth is the degree to which you can live free from fear.

Third, lavish grace on others. Choosing to give grace is easy to talk about. We do it all the time. Doing so in real life is another thing altogether. How different the world would be if we didn't compare, didn't take offense, didn't gossip about one another, and instead found ways to tangibly encourage and celebrate one another and give the benefit of the doubt during tough times.

Some of the best stories explore the intoxicating nature of grace. Victor Hugo's *Les Misérables* pits law against grace in the characters of Inspector Javert and Jean Valjean. Peter Shaffer's *Amadeus* explores the astounding musical talents of Mozart compared to his graceless contemporary Antonio Salieri. In both of these stories, one character must die because the two cannot coexist. Why? Because they are diametrically opposed to each other. Grace and judgment cannot occupy the same space. One must give way to the other. In *Les Misérables* the vengeful Javert takes his life. Valjean triumphs, and his spirit lives on. In *Amadeus,* Salieri survives Mozart, though the former all but loses his mind while Mozart's music still inspires.

If not welcomed, grace doesn't merely offend. It frustrates, angers, infuriates, and finally debilitates the rule keepers. Manning called this grace vulgar, because it "works without asking anything of us. It's not cheap. It's free, and as such will always be a banana peel for the orthodox foot and a fairy tale for the grown-up sensibility." Thankfully, as Manning further noted, "Grace is sufficient even though we huff and puff with all our might to try to find something or someone it cannot cover. Grace is enough. He is enough. Jesus is enough."[26]

Truth. Grace. Faith. Each is essential, and at times each is messy and raw. But they are real, tangible gifts, available to you and me.

Yet still so costly.

Too good to be true? Will our inspiration soon fizzle away as we step back into the drudgery of everyday life? There's always a cold wind just around the corner, right? Let's confront the notion of suffering, big and small, head-on.

Three

Kissing the Crucible

"What makes the desert beautiful," said the little prince, "is that somewhere it hides a well."

—Antoine de Saint-Exupéry

Recovering the truth about grace is a revolutionary step, one that will liberate your soul in ways you never dreamed. Our response to grace is joy—sheer joy, wild joy—not with boasting or flaunting a badge of honor, but, like children, with absolute wonder. To live authentically is to live in response to this magnificent, reckless grace. When we do, we encounter deep within our souls an infusion of the very substance God imparted to his Son when raising him from the dead.

Hard to believe? Yes, especially on Mondays. But true nonetheless.

Awesome, this mystery of grace.

Yet this mysterious grace often seems elusive in our human experience, and suffering is more commonplace. We all encounter the crucible of pain, great or small, acute or chronic, physical or emotional. Life slips off the rails. Death pays a visit. A relationship falters. Someone accuses. Blame or shame sets in. Wounds deepen and multiply. Along with our pain and suffering come honest questions. If grace is so good and so real and so free, then why must we suffer?

On January 12, 2010, at 4:53 in the afternoon, an earthquake shook the western side of the island of Hispaniola for thirty-five seconds, wreaking devastation upon the tiny nation of Haiti, the poorest country in the Western Hemisphere. Within hours of the tragedy, I boarded a five-seater plane, which was normally used for transporting bananas between the Bahamas and Florida, along with two French-speaking reporters. When we landed in Port-au-Prince, the capital of Haiti, the airport was dark and eerie. As we proceeded into the city, guttural cries of grief swept over us in waves. Bodies were strewn everywhere—children, mothers, fathers. The smell of death was inescapable. Many of those who survived refused to stay inside their homes, afraid the frequent tremors would bring their roofs down on their heads. To calm their trepidation, children sang songs to God, in both French and Creole, well into the night. Their voices, so beautiful, camouflaged the intense suffering around them.

Natural disasters are but one cause of suffering. War, genocide, human trafficking, and poverty also plague the world. With the constant stream of online news and social media, we are more aware of suffering than ever. The statistics are so common they fatigue us—nearly a billion hungry,[1] twenty-seven million slaves,[2] sixty million displaced,[3] and so on. But the people and their stories cannot be forgotten. I remember witnessing the desperation of a fifteen-year-old soldier after he realized the atrocities he had committed. I can still see the faces of young girls stolen from their families in Cambodia to be sold into slavery.

Suffering may be a global phenomenon, but it is also a personal experience. Almost everyone has suffered loss of one kind or another: a dream, a career, a relationship, or the life of a parent, friend, sibling, or child. Grief produces a silent suffering and, for some, a lifelong one. And physical suffering is more common than we think. Upward of one hundred million people in the United States alone live with chronic pain; that's almost one of every three people.[4]

When I ask people how they are really doing—it usually takes some gentle persistence to get the truth—I am amazed to discover how many people are suffering. "Tell me your sorrows," says Aslan in C. S. Lewis's Chronicles of Narnia.[5] Pain is ubiquitous and entirely familiar to the human condition. "Be kind, for everyone you meet is fighting a hard battle" holds an oft-quoted maxim. How true it is.

Our familiarity with pain leads to a question: If suffering is an inescapable part of the human experience, why do we do everything we can to avoid it? And when we can't, why do we hide our suffering?

SIDESTEPPING SORROW

Three years ago I received a frantic text message from my mother: "Emergency. Please call." My phone rang before I could place the call. It was my father. "Brenda is dead," he said between gasps for air.

My sister, Brenda, her husband, Lawrence, and their two children, Sammy, age six, and Audrey, age four, had just moved to Okinawa, Japan. Lawrence had joined the Judge Advocate General's Corps of the US Army as an attorney. Brenda was seven months pregnant with their

third child. In the middle of the night on May 20, Brenda awoke in a
sweat. She whispered to Lawrence that she was going downstairs to
turn on the air conditioner. Bolting awake an hour or so later, Lawrence
realized that Brenda had not returned to bed. He made his way toward
the stairs only to find my sister sprawled across the tiled landing, un-
conscious and bleeding from her forehead. Shocked, Lawrence tried to
resuscitate her, but it was too late. The hospital pronounced her dead on
arrival, and her unborn baby with her.

Brenda was an exceptional person who lived an extraordinary life.
She studied French literature in college and married her college sweet-
heart. Unfortunately, he became abusive, and after several years Brenda
found a way out of the marriage and joined the US Army. As a second
lieutenant, Brenda commanded a platoon in Iraq and later met and
married a fellow soldier, Lawrence, a compassionate, brilliant Jewish
man who later earned a Purple Heart for wounds sustained during a
Taliban ambush in Afghanistan. After finishing several tours with the
army, Brenda and Lawrence studied law at the University of Kansas.
Brenda also took a second degree, a master's in social work. While
studying law, Lawrence and Brenda began their family. Brenda even
found time to volunteer at a shelter for battered women.

Brenda's fall was named as the cause of her death, but she likely lost
consciousness at the top of the stairs due to a congenital heart defect
that wasn't discovered until the autopsy.

Brenda will always be my little sister; she and I were close. I only
wish I could tell her one more time that I love her.

—

Experiencing the death of a loved one is traumatic. Time screeches to a halt as emotions swing wildly from shock to denial to anger. As painful as death is, though, it can also bring new life. It has the power to permanently change you. It "lays bare what really matters," wrote Henri Nouwen.[6]

The first few weeks after a tragedy bring an overwhelming response of kindness, sympathy, and care from others. But that ends quickly. From there on, people tend to respond in one of three ways. Some ignore the pain. They either stay away or, if forced into your company, talk about anything but the person who died or how you are feeling—the things that are most important to you. Generally, these people are terrified of death, perhaps afraid a similar tragedy might befall them.

Then there are those who try to explain the tragedy. Some want to defend God by saying things like, "God works all things for good" or "Maybe God took Brenda because . . ." Others point to some rationale that is supposed to explain the reason behind the suffering. But all explanations fall flat. Some are even hurtful.

People in the third group, the smallest of the three, don't avoid death or try to explain it. They ask questions. They listen. They might even cry. Usually these people are personally acquainted with death in some way. They understand grief.

The people in all three groups are well intentioned. They don't realize we live in a culture that hides death and works hard to sanitize our daily lives from its pain. The elderly are hidden from sight in nursing homes. The terminally ill are confined to professional care centers or sequestered in hospital rooms, ideally with family but sometimes alone. We seldom come face to face with the aged, the sick, the dying.

When it comes to dealing with suffering, our culture is lost. Paul Brand, a surgeon who treated lepers in India, said:

> In the United States . . . I encountered a society that seeks to avoid pain at all costs. Patients lived at a greater comfort level than any I had previously treated, but they seemed far less equipped to handle suffering and far more traumatized by it.[7]

Our fear of suffering betrays a deeper belief. As a culture, we think of death as arbitrary or accidental, falling upon the unlucky. Many see suffering as punishment for something done wrong. Suffering carries a stigma; it makes us afraid; it reminds us of our vulnerability, our helplessness. So we hide it, and we hide from it.

All this leaves us without a coherent theology of suffering. Sure, we may have a theoretical treatment of it, a set of beliefs about the afterlife and maybe even an articulated purpose for suffering, but we have no practical theology of suffering. When it strikes, we have little to no coherent way of thinking about death or responding to it. Yet our theological heritage is quite profound on the subject of suffering. "Cyprian, Ambrose, and later Augustine made the case that Christians *suffered and died better*," wrote Timothy Keller, "and this was empirical, visible evidence that Christianity was 'the supreme philosophy.'"[8] It is odd, then, that when it comes to a practical, lived-out theology today, we are found wanting.

If we were to ask people on the street whether Christians accept suffering with more grace and patience than people without faith, what would they say? I doubt they would say we are known for dying better.

Like our culture in general, most of us live day to day as if suffering is to be absolutely avoided. Our fears have overtaken our theology on this point. We avoid the subject of death; we hide from its manifestations; we abhor illness, pain, and loneliness. We struggle to find purpose or meaning in suffering.

We are afraid.

HAPPY ARE THE SAD?

When I returned from Haiti after the earthquake, my son Joshua, who had just turned ten years old, asked, "Daddy, why did God let all those people die in Haiti?"

Joshua's question is, perhaps, the most salient question in human history: How can an all-loving and all-powerful God allow so much suffering in our world? Pastors say more people reject God because of suffering than any other reason. But they also say more people discover God during times of suffering than at any other time in their lives.[9]

What a paradox.

For some, the purpose behind suffering doesn't need to be explained. The fact that God chose to suffer with us is enough. Philosopher Peter Kreeft said the Christian God came to earth to deliberately put himself on the hook of human suffering.[10] Tim Keller noted that the fact we "can't see or imagine a good reason why God might allow something to happen doesn't mean there can't be one."[11] Compared with other faith traditions, "Christianity teaches that, contra fatalism, suffering is overwhelming; contra Buddhism, suffering is real; contra karma, suffering is often unfair; but contra secularism, suffering is meaningful," Keller wrote. "There is a purpose to it, and if faced rightly, it can drive us like a nail deep into the love of God and into more stability and spiritual power than you can imagine."[12]

Jesus talked a lot about suffering. More than that, he lived it. Jesus stepped into the world he created only to be vetoed by the very voices he had given breath to. He became poor and was oppressed by religion and government alike. And in the face of taunts and jeers, accusations and abandonment, scoffs and slaps, with the wounds of the world upon his shoulders, he said, "Father, forgive them, for they do not know what they are doing."[13] He answered one of the most fundamental and visceral questions of the human race "not in words but in deeds," said Kreeft.[14] God crucified himself. He suffered violence to overcome violence, he died to overturn death, and he suffered to ultimately overcome all suffering.

In the first century, suffering was generally viewed as a product of sin—sins of the sufferer or of generations past—or a manifestation of divine disapproval. That Jesus could triumph through suffering was a notion completely foreign in his day. In his Great Sermon, Jesus did something revolutionary. Rather than rejecting people who suffered, he praised them, conferring divine favor upon them. "Blessed are those who mourn," he said, "for they will be comforted."[15]

Like Jesus, the most vulnerable people in the world are acquainted with grief. Most families in Africa lose at least one child before age five from what Bono, rock star and founder of DATA (Debt AIDS Traffic Africa), calls "stupid poverty."[16] Fatal maladies that flourish in extreme poverty, such as respiratory disease, malnutrition, diarrhea, dehydration, or malaria, can be easily remedied. Death comes too easily to adults as well. Conflict, war, and terrorism claim millions of lives. Disease is rampant.

So how can the favor of God rest upon people who live so near death, who mourn so often?

I spend a lot of time connecting the very wealthy to the very poor. Compassion for the most vulnerable is generally viewed as a good thing across the world. But we seldom think of the favor of God resting on the vulnerable. Expecting to bless, we are surprised to be blessed by them.

In her 2009 TED Talk, Nigerian author Chimamanda Ngozi Adichie warned of the "danger of a single story." When we adopt a single narrative, we make it impossible to see a person or a country in any other way. If we hear only that someone is poor, for example, our response to the single story becomes one of pity, even if well intended. It becomes impossible to see that person as anything but poor. For many, the single story about Africa is "beautiful landscapes, beautiful animals, with incomprehensible people fighting senseless wars, dying from poverty and AIDS, unable to speak for themselves, and waiting to be saved by a kind, white foreigner," Adichie explained. "To create a single story, show a people as one thing, as only one thing, over and over again, and that is what they become," said Adichie.[17] Missing from much of Western literature and our discourse about Africa is the narrative of ingenuity, resilience, peace, faith, and friendship, all of which characterize much of the continent in beautiful array.

The first-century crowd listening to Jesus's sermon had likely pigeonholed the group Jesus was blessing into a single story. The poor, the mournful, the meek, the thirsty were down-and-out because they deserved it. Maybe their family was at fault. Or maybe God just didn't favor them. Only when we consider multiple stories can we begin to connect them. Multiple stories allow us to assemble a fuller picture, one that is usually closer to reality.

Interestingly, those who suffer are more likely to lavish grace on others. Why? They share an experience of pain and remember the stigma of a single story. From their shared perspective, they readily make room for another story; they give grace. Consider the woman who wept at Jesus's feet and dried his feet with her hair. She lived a life of suffering. Self-imposed? Yes, maybe, but her story was much bigger than a single narrative. Jesus saw into her soul. He dignified her. He forgave her. And because she was forgiven much, she loved much.[18]

What if suffering, for all its mystery, is a window into grace? What if those who mourn actually have a leg up on how to give freely, to lavish empathy, to love? And what if, as a result, they are happier? Referring to Martin Luther's theology of suffering, Keller said, "Suffering dispels the illusion that we have the strength and competence to rule our own lives and save ourselves. People 'become nothing through suffering' so that they can be filled with God and his grace."[19]

Becoming nothing, now that's something to aspire to, right?

But what if becoming nothing, simply letting go or laying down your life for God, is not essentially about giving up or giving in, feeling grief or pain or admitting failure, but is rather a grand pathway to freedom, to grace, to authentic faith, to something so extraordinary we struggle even to conceive of it? What if suffering, regardless of its cause, is a tangible extension of God's grace precisely because it functions as an invitation to something more, something grand, something other? I've experienced God's presence most when I've suffered.

He is especially near in our pain, offering a handwritten invitation to something . . .

More.

HOW EVIL BECKONS GRACE

Before we continue our conversation, I owe you a few practical principles. *First, evil is evil; we must always seek to confront it.* C. S. Lewis said it best:

> Christianity is a fighting religion. It thinks God made the
> world—that space and time, heat and cold, and all the colours
> and tastes, and all the animals and vegetables, are things that
> God "made up out of His head" as a man makes up a story. But
> it also thinks that a great many things have gone wrong with the
> world that God made and that God insists, and insists very
> loudly, on our putting them right again.[20]

Second, evil is much closer to all of us than we usually think. God asks us to consider how we all have fallen short of his will and how to overcome our sin. *Forgive us our sins and help us to forgive others,* we pray, as well as, *Deliver us from evil.*[21]

Russian novelist Alexander Solzhenitsyn raised global awareness of the Soviet Union's inhumane system of forced labor camps, which operated from 1918 to 1956. Of the nearly 15 million people incarcerated in the gulag system during a twenty-five-year period, at least 1.5 million died. Some estimate the number as three times that many. Half of all political prisoners were never given a trial. Solzhenitsyn was one of them. In his well-known work *The Gulag Archipelago,* Solzhenitsyn reflects on the nature of evil:

> It was only when I lay there on rotting prison straw that I sensed within myself the first stirrings of good. Gradually it was disclosed to me that the line separating good and evil passes not through states, nor between classes, nor between political parties either—but right through every human heart—and through all human hearts. This line shifts. Inside us, it oscillates with the years. And even within the hearts overwhelmed with evil, one small bridgehead of good is retained. And even in the best of all hearts, there remains . . . an unuprooted small corner of evil. . . .
>
> If only there were evil people somewhere insidiously committing evil deeds, and it were necessary only to separate them from the rest of us and destroy them. But the line dividing good and evil cuts through the heart of every human being. And who is willing to destroy a piece of his own heart?[22]

We are all on a journey to overcome the enemy within, the evil that lurks in our hearts. Grace is our remedy, and love, our goal.

Third, sometimes suffering is the direct result of evil, but God can always redeem it. In the Old Testament, Joseph suffered at the hands of his brothers. Tired of his dreams and jealous of their father's favoritism, the brothers threw Joseph into a pit, then trafficked him. As a result, Joseph suffered for years, both as a slave and, later, in prison. Through a series of divine miracles, Joseph was eventually elevated to viceroy of

Egypt. When his brothers came to seek his help concerning a famine in their land, he hid himself from them and wept.[23] Ultimately, he revealed himself to them, saying,

> "Don't be afraid. Am I in the place of God? You intended to
> harm me, but God intended it for good to accomplish what is
> now being done, the saving of many lives. So then, don't be
> afraid. I will provide for you and your children." And he
> reassured them and spoke kindly to them.[24]

For Joseph, God redeemed his brothers' evil with good.

So it is with us. We don't always know the causes behind our suffering. Suffering often appears to be random, senseless evil. Sometimes it is just that. Even so, *all* suffering is redeemable, which is why God invites us to participate in his freedom-giving grace.

ABOUT THAT CRUCIBLE

Have you encountered someone who exhibited extraordinary grace during a season of intense or chronic suffering?

A filmmaker friend who had all but thrown in the towel on faith traveled with me and a few others to Congo just a few months after a surge in violence in that country. After meeting with several women who told us of their suffering and described how they had forgiven the perpetrators, my friend made this stunning statement: "I don't believe in the God of the United States, but I believe in the God of Congo." He had encountered people who spoke a profound message through their lives: "God is with us in our suffering, and that is enough. We believe." For him, it took a journey into the heart of suffering to glimpse the heart of a loving God.[25]

Encountering grace in the lives of those who suffer has changed me too—often profoundly. These experiences are wells from which I drink. We, too, can be wells of life when we experience the crucible of suffering. Instead of resisting, blaming, or fighting—all of which are normal responses in everyday life—we can purposefully accept the experience of suffering, embracing the wisdom we can gain from it without justifying its cause or trying to neatly explain the reasons for it. When we accept suffering, trusting that we will emerge from its crucible with more grace, more humility, and more love, we live out a theology of suffering that is rare, especially in the West. The idea that we can kiss the crucible, that we can make suffering an intimate friend, is a notion as old as our faith, but it is reserved for those willing to view suffering as an unlikely teacher, yet one dripping with wisdom.

But let's be honest. When we suffer, poetry doesn't help much. How do we learn to kiss the crucible?

First, do your best to embrace suffering, difficult though that may be. Years ago I spent some time with a friend who tends cattle as an avocation. One day we drove out to one of his fields, where he showed me a young horse, a foal born just a few weeks before. He spoke kindly to the horse, then leaned down alongside it and gently wrapped his arms around its front and back legs in a bear-hug fashion. The colt jumped and struggled for a few moments but then finally relaxed into my friend's arms as it began to trust him.

Pain can be like that bear hug. It's normal to resist pain; alleviating pain is always the right thing to do. Seeking help might take the pain away. Prayer might help us overcome. But often the pain remains, doesn't it? That's when we must recognize that God's love hasn't changed—that *he* hasn't changed—and that we can trust him in the midst of suffering.

Second, don't blame yourself. If your suffering is the result of your own actions, by all means take responsibility for it, but avoid self-blame and the shame that comes with it. Too often we fall prey to a false version of faith that correlates suffering with mistakes, poor choices, or personal sin. We do live in a world governed largely by the law of cause and effect, but Jesus refutes the notion that suffering is axiomatic proof of a badly lived life. For example, in Jesus's day, a tower fell and killed eighteen people. People apparently drew the conclusion that those eighteen were "worse offenders than all the others who lived in Jerusalem." But Jesus emphatically repudiated that idea and the logic behind it.[26]

Third, make suffering your teacher. While we may not understand why we go through seasons of suffering, we can allow them to shape our lives. God is very near during times of suffering. Someone said, "The darker the night, the brighter the stars. The deeper the grief, the closer is God."[27] Suffering may very well be your invitation to understand the love of God in ways you could not have fathomed before. Others need you to show them the way.

Finally, be honest about your journey. We too often talk only about success in our faith communities. We avoid honest conversations about our challenges. We hide our suffering. Perhaps we feel ashamed or without favor. Or maybe we don't know how to be vulnerable. Worse, perhaps our community doesn't allow vulnerability. In an interview with Eugene Peterson, Bono praised the raw, brutal honesty, sorrow, or confusion displayed in the psalms.[28] The singer said that he finds a lot of dishonesty in Christian art and exhorted artists to

> write a song about their bad marriage. Write a song about how they are pissed off . . . because that's what God wants from you—the truth . . . and that truthfulness will set you free. . . . Why I am suspicious of Christians is because of this lack of realism. And I'd love to see more of that—in art and in life and in music.[29]

For all the mystery surrounding suffering—its causes, asymmetry, and purpose—there are moments when we glimpse the heart of God. For example, in a quiet corner of Boston Common, just off the tourist path, you can find a monument to the discovery of ether. On one side of this tall obelisk are these words: "Neither shall there be any more pain," a quote from the book of Revelation.[30] On the opposite side is a quote from the prophet Isaiah, "This also comes from the Lord of Hosts who is wonderful in counsel and excellent in working."[31] William Thomas Green Morton, a dentist from Massachusetts who trained in Baltimore, first demonstrated the use of ether as an inhaled surgical anesthetic. His epithet reads:

> Inventor and Revealer of Inhalation Anesthesia:
> Before Whom, in All Time, Surgery was Agony;
> By Whom, Pain in Surgery was Averted and Annulled;
> Since Whom, Science has Control of Pain.[32]

The date was 1846, the year in which surgery was refined, sparing millions from the agony that all before them had endured. That the God of the universe would reveal the properties of ether to humankind says we serve a God who is ultimately committed to overcoming our suffering. One day all suffering will end. The promise is clear, and our hearts crave it. We long for that day. But in the meantime, on this side of eternity, kissing our crucibles will awaken us to the astounding nature of grace. And as we encounter grace through suffering, we are drawn close to the heart of the living God.

Grace and suffering are inextricably linked to form a bedrock of truth: that God's grace is available to the least likely people and in the least likely ways. This truth comes furiously knocking, in surprising ways, calling you and me to rise above our fear.

But there is a raison d'être, a reason for it all, a grand purpose, a chief motive behind the universe, the consummation of grace, and the substance of suffering.

To this we now turn.

Part 2

LOVE

What you are in love with,
what seizes your imagination,
will affect everything.
It will decide
what will get you out of bed in the morning,
what you do with your evenings,
how you spend your weekends,
what you read,
whom you know,
what breaks your heart,
and what amazes you with joy and gratitude.
Fall in love,
stay in love,
and it will decide everything.

—Pedro Arrupe

Four

Divine and Dusty

The idea that there's a force of love and
logic behind the universe . . . that . . .
would choose to describe itself as a
baby born in . . . poverty is genius, and
brings me to my knees.

—Bono

I f grace is the quintessential truth and the crucible of suffering an invitation to apprehend that truth, then love is its proof.

I am not talking about just any kind of love. The versions we encounter in the mall or on the screen or through social media are not, in the end, comparable to this love. No, I am talking about the kind of love that astonishes, that endures, that risks, that joyfully sacrifices. It permanently changes us, and it holds the explosive power to redefine the world. This kind of love results when we gulp large doses of grace and find the courage to kiss the crucible of suffering. This love belongs to God, is endemic to his nature and character, and manifests in tangible, real, efficacious action.

Such love flourishes only when it's anchored in real life, with all its drudgery and challenges, joys and sorrows. In order for love to be divine, it must first get dusty.

For the last several years, Belinda and I have spent New Year's Day in Washington DC with close friends Andy and Sunita. They are the kind of friends we are not tempted to impress. They are authentic, earthy people with open hearts and generous spirits, who inspire and seek to be inspired. They freely love, without qualification or condition. And they judge their own faith by real measures—by what they do as much as what they say, by the depth of their relationships, and by the character they see and discover in each other.

But they live at full tilt. They are raising three kids under the age of three. Their first two, Gabe and Addie, were initially fostered and then adopted, and their youngest, Asha, was a beautiful surprise. Our time together is always punctuated by a shriek or two, boisterous laughter, and several rounds of tears—sometimes by the adults as well as the kids! These visits are refreshing but always anchored in real life—messy life, the good, the bad, the ugly, and the necessary.

Our friends help us keep our faith authentic. They help us learn how to love.

David Bosch said that the church must become "an inseparable union of the divine and the dusty."[1] Too often we siphon the messiness of life away from what we consider spiritual when, instead, the profane and the sacred are meant to walk together, arms locked and friendly.

The problem we face is something more than mere dualism however. By relegating our faith to a building or service or a single day of the week, we bypass its essential quality—ordinariness. On Sunday we herald grace as a distinguishing characteristic of our faith. On Monday we often encounter a different experience altogether. Competition, offense, isolation, undercutting, and indifference mark our daily lives. The spiritual life is not usually tested inside a church or during a Bible study. Most people can pull it together for an hour or two a week. Living and working with others throughout the week is different. We can't be at our best every day. We can't hide our flaws from someone who knows us well.

Our rhetoric about love sounds wonderful, yet we often can't seem to put it into practice. Unlike grace, which requires revelation, love requires demonstration—tangible expressions of compassion through everyday actions, not just words. Think of the people who have affected your life the most. Likely they are the ones who showed you love in some definitive, substantial, memorable way.

PITCHING A TENT

God made his love tangible when he dressed in human skin and "made his dwelling among us."[2] The Greek word translated as "dwelling" is from a root word that means "to encamp, to pitch one's tent,"[3] which was a fitting metaphor for first-century Bethlehem, a working-class town that had swelled with people registering for a census demanded by Caesar Augustus.

People spoke of the Romans in hushed voices for fear of reprisal. Incidents of injustice filled the news. Oppression ruled the day.

The first Christmas wasn't happy; it was chaos.

The story begins with Herod, the king of Judea, who rose to power through political scheming. During his reign he murdered his wife and his wife's mother and slaughtered children in Bethlehem. Caesar Augustus, Herod's patron and the emperor of Rome, was a tyrant too. Augustus was the adopted son of Julius Caesar, the first emperor Rome declared a god, making Augustus the son of a god. Rome under Augustus dealt with opposition harshly, and both lawbreakers and dissidents were regularly crucified along the well-traveled roads of Judea. Innocent people were oppressed, and some Romans sold their own children into slavery.[4] Such was life under the Pax Romana, or Roman Peace.

Amid this suffering and injustice, amid the oppression and the fear, among the cries of forgotten people, God announces to a few surprising people he's about to pitch his tent. And what do we hear in response?

Singing, actually.

Mary sings, "He has brought down rulers from their thrones but has lifted up the humble." Zechariah sings, "He has come to his people and redeemed them . . . from our enemies and from the hand of all who hate us." And a chorus of angels sing, "On earth peace . . ."[5]

Three songs, each revolutionary, each a song of deliverance. Mary? She could have been enslaved for her seditious lyrics. Zechariah? Executed for his. The chorus of angels declaring peace at the high tide of the Pax Romana? Treason. Gabriel, proclaiming the birth of the "Son of the Most High"[6] in the land of Augustus, the son of god? An attempted coup d'état, punishable by death.

In the first-century world, saturated with pain and injustice, a light dawned. God pitched his tent among an unlikely pair, a peasant mother and trembling father. The Son of God came as a defenseless child, born on the periphery of the world. His plan? To overcome a world of violent suffering by living a life of sacrificial love. This outrageous wonder, that the divine would get his feet dirty amid the violence, oppression, and suffering of his people, came as an extravagant surprise to shock a ragged world.

Theologians call the divine descent from heaven to earth the incarnation. God dressing in human skin, emptying himself of his full array of glory and power, is called "kenosis":

> Though he was in the form of God, did not count equality with God a thing to be grasped, but emptied himself, by taking the form of a servant, being born in the likeness of men. And being found in human form, he humbled himself by becoming obedient to the point of death, even death on a cross.[7]

Most scholars would say that there is no greater summary of the humility of God. The kenosis demonstrates God's altruism, his love made manifest, tangible, real.

Stunning.

Scholars have recently challenged the translation of the first line of this text. For years we read it as, "Although he was in the form of God, he did not count equality with God a thing to be grasped," implying that the incarnation was an exception to God's normal way of doing things. Michael Gorman, a noted Pauline scholar, translates the text this way: "*Because* he was in the form of God . . ." rather than "Although he was in the form of God . . . ,"[8] which suggests the kenosis was "not [just] a passing exercise in ultimate obedience, but a permanent revelation about the nature of God."[9]

God's nature is humble, self-emptying, sacrificial—not just once, but for all time.

Would anyone have staged God's entrance into the world as a baby? That God would pitch his tent in the squalor of Bethlehem; that he would commission a heavenly chorus to announce joy to, of all people, shepherds; that he would summon a few sages from beyond the empire, and beyond his culture, to bend their knees says to us that God dwells in unlikely places with unlikely people. Our God doesn't remain distant but instead finds his home among the brokenhearted.

Jesus the helpless child, the sojourner, the stranger to many, the sometime vagabond, the one-time refugee—do we really want to follow that example? Is it even possible? Why can't we leave the notion of kenosis and, for that matter, the idea of living a "dusty" life to God?

"The paradox of the Christian community," said Henri Nouwen, "is that people are gathered together in voluntary displacement." The term *voluntary displacement* implies a kenosis of our own, in which we willingly let go of security and move beyond the "prevalent norms and values" around us. Nouwen clarifies the phrase:

> In voluntary displacement, we cast off the illusion of "having it
> together" and thus begin to experience our true condition, which
> is that we, like everyone else, are pilgrims on the way, sinners in
> need of grace. Through voluntary displacement, we counteract
> the tendency to become settled in false comfort and to forget the
> fundamentally unsettled position that we share with all people.
> Voluntary displacement leads us to the existential recognition of
> our inner brokenness and thus brings us to a deeper solidarity
> with the brokenness of our fellow human beings.[10]

Maybe stepping into the wake of God's kenosis isn't so implausible after all.

BLESSED ARE THE MEEK

In his Sermon on the Mount, Jesus said, "Blessed are the meek, for they will inherit the earth."[11] We normally do not associate being meek, mild, or gentle with power. But Jesus showed a different way. He was born to peasants in an off-the-path blue-collar town. He never attended formal school. He held no political office. He didn't manipulate the crowds toward revolution (though he could have), and he didn't resist his accusers.

But meekness is not synonymous with weakness. For Jesus, being meek didn't mean the lack of strength but rather strength under authority, his Father's authority. The Greek word for *meek* (*praus*) means exercising strength with humility, gentleness, and even restraint, all of which require a deep level of trust.[12] This is not what we normally think of when we think of power. In the first century, few would have thought the power of God would be delivered with meekness. Today we may naturally shy away from a God who is meek. But meek is not weak.

Through the prophet Isaiah, God said, "Once more I will astound these people with wonder upon wonder."[13] But not the kind of wonder we normally think of.

Emmanuel, God with us, entered fully into life. He wept with those who wept. He validated suffering, but he also protested against it, not with the conventional means of politics, military might, or insurrection, but by pitching his tent alongside those who experienced it. He associated himself with anyone willing to reach out with simple faith.

When God put on human flesh, he redefined power. He comforted, healed, redeemed, and restored, often quietly but always with authority. The inversion of power in Jesus's life is counterintuitive, confounding, and stunning, yet still strong, awesome, and convincing.

Jesus was shockingly, amazingly, and beautifully . . .

Meek.

Is there an answer for the grieving mother whose child has succumbed to hunger or the community splintered by brutality or the father who is prevented from planting a crop because of war? Is there an answer for you and me and for our children and friends who struggle through life, who experience disillusionment with faith or a derailed career or a relationship or dreams that have been delayed yet again?

"Blessed are the meek," Jesus said, "for they will inherit the earth."

Because Jesus paid attention to those suffering on the margins, we should too. After all, the meek will inherit the earth. Someone has said, "It's not the millions that move us, but the one." The crisis in Syria has certainly proven this true. *Washington Post* columnist Michael Gerson captured the words of Syrian children stranded in Lebanon: "My home is all broken in Syria," said a little girl. "A rocket came and hit my father in the head," said another. One boy drew a picture of a bomb.[14]

My friends and colleagues in Syria, Jordan, Iraq, and Turkey are exhausted from responding to the escalating crisis. They have pitched their tents in what is being called the worst humanitarian crisis since World War II. And we know that millions more around the world are refugees, bringing the total to more than sixty million people.[15] We are living in an age of an unprecedented movement of people, a global exodus.

People across the world are following the example of Jesus by answering the biblical call to welcome the stranger,[16] an indispensable ethic for anyone choosing to follow Jesus of Nazareth, who once set out on the refugee trail himself. Churches are coming together to support refugees in the Middle East. Compassion has also spilled over to the millions fleeing war in places including South Sudan, Congo, and Yemen.

Yet fear rises in us when we talk about welcoming Syrians or Iraqis here in the United States. Many are concerned about creating a gateway for terrorism. While that fear is understandable, it steals our compassion.[17] We are left paralyzed, unable to demonstrate love. Fear causes us to pack up our tents and retreat from the dusty, sometimes violent, world.

When we do, we forget that the global exodus is personal and includes each one of us. We all have our own stories as immigrants or refugees, whether as first-generation migrants or as those who are several generations removed. I recently found my wife, Belinda, staring at a photo of her grandfather, Alexis Koshanov, or Grandpa Alex, as Belinda knew him. Alexis fled Lithuania just before Hitler's whisper campaign but was turned away at Ellis Island because he was Jewish.[18] He later immigrated to the United States via Canada, but his sister died in Auschwitz, and his brother barely survived Dachau. Today's global migration reminded Belinda of her family's exodus from Europe not long ago. "I am a refugee, just two generations removed," she said, tears filling her eyes.

When we realize that we, too, are immigrants, even if a generation or so removed, it's much easier to open our hearts to welcome others. Almost every day I hear about a church, neighborhood, or community opening their arms to a refugee family. These people are heroes. Why?

Because they have chosen to pitch their tents among refugees. As they do, the terms *refugee* and *immigrant* quickly give way to *brother* and *sister* and, often, *American.* "These people are friends," my associates tell me.

We are at our best not when we turn our backs, demand our rights, and talk of building walls but when we welcome the refugee, the sojourner, the immigrant. We are at our best—as a people, a church, a community, and a nation—not when we fear but when we love with gentle strength.

Blessed are the meek.

Aiding refugees is but one example of how we can pitch our tents with the vulnerable. A couple of months ago I couldn't sleep because I was thinking about what it would be like to be a follower of Jesus in South Sudan. I was thinking of a father who watched his three young sons bleed to death after government soldiers castrated them. I thought about another father who watched soldiers tie his children together and burn them alive in their home.

Some are saying South Sudan will soon become a failed state unless something changes. In my opinion the state has already failed its people. All this began when South Sudan's president, Salva Kiir, got into a power struggle with Riek Machar, the vice president. Their fight quickly turned tribal; Kiir is Dinka, and Machar is Nuer. The country split along ethnic lines, and violence became rampant. Diplomacy has failed, perhaps because some of the conveners from East Africa are not neutral concerning the conflict.

I have been working in humanitarian aid for more than two decades. I wish I could say that compassion is impartial, but that usually is not the case. Compassion follows the money, and the money tends to follow CNN. But we don't have to wait for cable news to take notice of a problem in order to take action. If tens of thousands of people all across our country begin praying for South Sudan each week, compassion will rise. If people like you and me begin asking the simple question "Where is the outrage?" on social media, we might see a groundswell of interest that could influence others, including the press and governments, to do something for our brothers and sisters who are acutely suffering. We can pitch our tent in South Sudan.

We love best when we are willing to get dusty.

POSTMODERN FOOT WASHING

Speaking of dust, near the end of his life, Jesus "got up from the meal, took off his outer clothing, and wrapped a towel around his waist. After that, he poured water into a basin and began to wash his disciples' feet, drying them with the towel that was wrapped around him."[19] And just when the disciples thought they were off the hook—after all, foot washing was a slave's job in their day—Jesus said,

> Now that I, your Lord and Teacher, have washed your feet, you
> also should wash one another's feet. I have set you an example
> that you should do as I have done for you.[20]

Apart from the times Pope Francis has washed the feet of prisoners or refugees or women, I am not a fan of modern-day foot washing. It's generally awkward, no matter how well it's done. And despite the well-intended metaphor, the act of foot washing doesn't translate easily into our postmodern lives.

Instead of literally washing one another's feet, we must transpose the meaning of this dusty divinity into everyday life. The question to ask is this: What needs in our culture are generally left to servants or left unattended altogether?

I can think of a few. Doing the dishes, of course, or cleaning the bathroom. And what about giving attention to people who have been kicked around for so long that they're virtually impossible to talk with, whose behavior may merit no niceties whatsoever? Or what about those who need their souls washed with forgiveness—your forgiveness—and who may never acknowledge, let alone reciprocate, your gift?

Years ago Belinda and I visited a group of American students who were living in Poland. They were seeking to befriend young Poles in a rather tough part of town. To save on living costs, our students chose to share an apartment with three locals who happened to be living a rather wild life, including drinking binges and sex parties late into the night.

Our students told us how they were making the best of it. They told a few stories that were modestly hopeful. Yet we could tell they were really struggling. Some of them pulled Belinda aside and said they were mortified to use the shared shower because it was the primary venue for the late-night sex escapades of their flat mates. Belinda took a look. They were right; it was disgusting.

The team set off for an evening event, and Belinda and I had an hour or two to kill before leaving for the train station. Belinda suggested we clean the shower. (Notice it was her idea, not mine!) I offered a few reasons why it might be better if we left earlier for the train, but I knew Belinda was right. For that particular day in Lublin, Poland, scrubbing a shower was the best way to demonstrate love for our team.

Sometimes foot washing doesn't involve feet at all.

LOVE SUPREME

After having washed his disciples' feet, just before celebrating the first Eucharist, Jesus gave his disciples a new mandate:

> A new command I give you: Love one another. As I have loved
> you, so you must love one another. By this everyone will know
> that you are my disciples, if you love one another.[21]

I recently met with an esteemed leader of the Assyrian Church in northern Iraq. During our conversation he mentioned a comment by an Iraqi Muslim official about Christianity in Iraq, which has its roots in the first century. He said, "We know you are not a true faith because you don't love each other."

Ouch.

I wonder how differently the world would see Jesus if we could "differ in how we differ."[22]

Someone has said Desmond Tutu was "the only figure holding back a tide of violence" in South Africa during apartheid. What would Tutu say to us about the tensions we are experiencing today?

Tutu centered his life and thought around the idea of *ubuntu,* the plural form of the African word *bantu,* meaning "humanness." In his day apartheid separated people from one another according to race. Ubuntu unifies, harmonizes, and brings people together. According to Tutu, while we maintain our uniqueness as individuals, our together-ness defines us. "My humanity is bound up in yours for we can only be human together," said Tutu.[23]

Tutu's ubuntu was a theology of love. He sought forgiveness and reconciliation between the oppressor and oppressed, proposing a new community for rebuilding the society. Once, during a riot that erupted during a political funeral, he thwarted the death of a policeman by throwing himself across the man's body as he was being stoned. "Let not the enemy divide us . . . let us not be filled with a desire for revenge," said Tutu.[24] He envisioned liberation through nonviolent resistance, which would foster reconciliation and restore

> the oppressor's humanity by releasing and enabling the op-
> pressed to see their oppressors as peers under God. In this can
> be a mutual understanding, as Jesus teaches, through friend-
> ship. . . . The relationship of oppressor and oppressed and the
> resulting definition of humanity through racial classification are
> broken through *ubuntu,* an alternative way of being in a hostile
> world.[25]

Tutu proposed a "new humanity" to which all people would rise, a humanity that required mutual respect, a humanity that required all races, both majority and minority, to contribute equally to creating a new future. Once reconciled and liberated, people would create "deli-cate networks of interdependence" across the plurality of belief and the diversity of race:

> Ubuntu refers to the person who is welcoming, who is hospi-
> table, who is warm and generous, who is affirming of others,
> who does not feel threatened . . . [who] has a proper self-
> assurance that comes from knowing they belong to a greater
> whole, and . . . are diminished when another is humiliated . . .

is tortured, is oppressed, is treated as if they were less than who they are. What a wonderful world it can be, it will be, when we know that our destinies are linked inextricably to one another's.[26]

Desmond Tutu lives a faith that is both divine and dusty.

My humanity is bound up in my brothers and sisters here in the United States, in faith communities torn by racial tension or xenophobia, and across the world. Why? Because we need one another in order to be human. The apostle Paul said it this way: "If one part suffers, every part suffers with it; if one part is honored, every part rejoices with it."[27] Your problem is my problem too.

Faith loses its meaning when it's not anchored in dusty life. Unless we involve ourselves in the problems of the world—whether down the road, across the hallway, or around the globe—our faith becomes shallow, superficial, unconvincing, and even shrill or clangy, like Paul's cymbal in 1 Corinthians 13. "Someone will say, 'You have faith; I have deeds,'" said James. "Show me your faith without deeds, and I will show you my faith by what I do."[28]

When it comes to whom we love, faith, expressing itself in love, knows no boundaries. How we love matters.

But who we love matters even more.

Five

Wing Tips and Flip-Flops

I wonder how many people I've looked at all my
life and never seen.

—John Steinbeck

Every year in February members of Congress convene an event in
Washington DC called the National Prayer Breakfast. Heads of
state, clergy, celebrities, and athletes attend. A famous musician sings.
Someone gives a keynote address. The president addresses the crowd.

While the Prayer Breakfast is typical Washington fare, sometimes
the event makes headlines.

In 1994 Mother Teresa said, "I am willing to accept any child who
would be aborted and to give that child to a married couple who will
love the child and be loved by the child."[1] The crowd jumped to its feet,
but the president and First Lady remained seated. A decade later Bono
stunned the audience when he said, "God is in the slums, in the card-
board boxes where the poor play house. . . . God is in the silence of a

mother who has infected her child with a virus that will end both their lives. . . . God is in the cries heard under the rubble of war. . . . God is in the debris of wasted opportunity and lives, and God is with us if we are with them."[2] The room sat silent. More recently Ben Carson confronted the president on certain policy matters, to the surprise of many. Four years later Carson launched his own presidential campaign.

Not surprisingly, when the president and First Lady are in the room, the Secret Service keeps a close watch on who enters and leaves. So it's customary for hundreds of people to make a beeline for the restrooms just after the couple departs. (Human biology, it seems, doesn't respect pomp and circumstance!) Several years ago Belinda slipped in a selfie with Tim Tebow before grabbing me to follow her to the restrooms. While waiting in line with scores of people, most of them glued to their smartphones, I couldn't help but ask myself what Jesus would think of the illustrious event we were attending. If he were there, in the flesh, would he celebrate the fact that so many important people were taking a few moments to pray? Would he nod approval during the songs of praise? Would he admonish the crowd, like Mother Teresa or Bono, for not doing enough for children or the poor? Or maybe he wouldn't attend at all, finding more important things to do. Worse still, maybe he wouldn't be invited in the first place.

As I pondered my questions, regrettably with a hint of smugness, a waiter threw back a nearby door and gave me a clear view into the kitchen. Before the door swung shut, I glimpsed the underbelly of one of the largest hotels in Washington DC, where several thousand meals were prepared—scrambled eggs, bite-size servings of quiche, yogurt parfaits—and where hundreds of hotel staff members, many of them first- or second-generation immigrants, darted to and fro like bees attending their queen. The scene froze in my mind as I grappled with a singular thought:

If Jesus were here, he'd be in the kitchen.

Call it an epiphany, a moment of inspiration, a lofty idea, a timely conviction.

Or maybe it was God.

During the second century, Christians in certain cities of the Roman Empire were commonly known as "the third race." Romans and Greeks were deemed the first race and Jews the second. But the mixing of the two and the addition of foreigners was thought to have created a separate race altogether. One of the earliest church fathers, Tertullian, writing around the year 200, said that this designation for Christians "was perfectly common on the lips of pagans in Carthage." Tacitus, the Roman historian, said Christians were "vain and insane," called them "reprobate," and blamed them for their "hatred of the human race."[3]

Yet this scornful designation soon became a term of honor among Christians.

The third race shocked the Roman Empire not because Gentiles or Jews were following a foreign God but because they were violating the social norms of the day. They were upsetting the class structure in offensive ways. Jewish rabbis and Roman soldiers who had chosen to follow Christ were sharing meals together. Masters and slaves were praying together. Women participated in worship.

In the culture of the day, the third race was a sociological impossibility.

The National Prayer Breakfast, with its bold focus on prayer in a city where faith is increasingly marginalized, serves an important role in our civic life. Laudable though it may be, the event falls far short of creating a sociological impossibility. The servant class—the hotel wait-staff—is separate from those in attendance. And the attendees, forming a sort of upper middle class, are mostly separated from the powerful and famous people who conduct the event.

Data shows us that Sunday morning continues to be the most segregated hour of the week. Author and friend Ed Stetzer noted,

> Surprisingly, most churchgoers are content with the ethnic status quo in their churches. In a world where our culture is increasingly diverse, and many pastors are talking about diversity, it appears most people are happy where they are—and with whom they are.[4]

We might cite a few exceptions, but my observation is that the North American church as a whole does not qualify as a sociological impossibility either. Most of us experience a church consisting of what D. A. Carson calls "natural friends" not "natural enemies." While natural friendship is a good thing, this version of Sunday morning is a far cry from the second-century church.

When the apostle Paul spoke of the ideal Christian community, he used the Greek word *koinonia,* indicating a shared life in Christ. *Koinonia* was a common word in Greek culture. Pythagoras used it to describe a society where "all things were held in common for all."[5] Paul redefined the concept to include God. Then Paul pushed the idea further. He said if you have koinonia with "the Spirit, if any tenderness and compassion, then make my joy complete by being like-minded, having the same love, being one in spirit and of one mind."[6] By inviting the

early faith communities to koinonia, Paul exhorted them to press beyond the conventional categories of the day and become societies where
there was "neither Jew nor Gentile, neither slave nor free, nor . . . male
and female."[7] Their shared life would even include their former enemies
as well as the marginalized and the unrecognized. It would be a "fellowship of differents" in the words of Scot McKnight.[8] D. A. Carson summarized it well:

> What binds us together is not common education, common
> race, common income levels, common politics, common
> nationality, common accents, common jobs, or anything else
> of that sort. Christians come together . . . because they have
> all been saved by Jesus Christ. . . .
> . . . Christian love . . . is . . . mutual love among social
> incompatibles.[9]

So often, however, we experience anything but a community of
differents. We experience the principle of "homogenous unity" instead,
the tendency for people to be more open to faith when they "cross few
or no racial, linguistic, or class barriers."[10] Turning differents, let alone
enemies, into friends can seem idealistic, romantic, or even dangerous.
How can we possibly live out such a sociological impossibility? Perhaps
the more important question is this: Why would we want to?

Precisely. If we are honest, most of us would admit that we really
don't want to join a community of differents. It's awkward at best and
daunting at worst. Fear is often the underlying cause of our reluctance,
whether we are conscious of it or not. Sometimes the fear is subtle. We
dread the unfamiliar. And sometimes the fear has a more obvious root.

It's too much work, too messy, too labor-intensive, too risky to be involved with others.

But when we overcome that fear, something astonishing happens. If you could experience an authentic community of differents, one in which people of varying socioeconomic and ethnic backgrounds, even theologies, genuinely come together, it would surprise you.

SOCIOLOGICAL IMPOSSIBILITIES

Years ago Belinda and I lived aboard one of the world's largest nongovernmental hospital ships. Also aboard were people of more than thirty nationalities, representing Europe, Africa, Asia, Australia, New Zealand, the Pacific Islands, the Caribbean, and the Americas, from some thirty-five faith traditions. After touring the ship a former United Nations official turned to me with a puzzled expression and said, "This really shouldn't work, you know."

His comment surprised me. Yes, day-to-day shipboard life with some four hundred crewmates felt messy. There were disagreements, some turning into full-blown conflicts. And there were certainly differences in theology, lifestyle, and politics. But conflicts were generally resolved, opinions usually sharpened one another, and for many the ship's voyage became a journey of discovery. No matter the tensions throughout the week, by Friday night on the aft deck of the ship, we were laughing again. What seemed impossible to my UN friend was lived out every day.

I realize now that our community was possible because of the presence of an overwhelming grace—thick, tangible grace. And there were other elements that paved the way for this sociological impossibility. We were tenaciously committed to a common vision. United by a call to serve, we contributed our unique strengths while sacrificing for, and with, people who suffered far more than we did. This shared purpose provided a baseline of trust upon which we formed an unwritten social contract. Implicitly we all knew that we'd fight for our collective vision. And that fight was waged with unlikely weapons—humility, forgiveness, and vulnerability.

Years later I realized how rare these aspects of community life really are, even in the best of faith communities.

There was one other essential element, one that I've been searching for ever since. Somehow we learned to judge one another less. Suspending judgment—along with all its associated maladies, such as comparison, criticism, insecurity, and shame—freed our community to become something greater than the sum of its parts.

But how can members of a community rid themselves of the sometimes overwhelming impulse to judge one another?

JETTISONING JUDGMENT

When most people consider faith or religion, especially Evangelicalism, "judgmental" is usually one of the first descriptors that come to mind. As novelist Tami Hoag wrote, "We never know the quality of someone else's life, though we seldom resist the temptation to assume and pass judgment."[11] Ouch. What an indictment, especially since the heart of the gospel and the life of Jesus[12] are anything but judgmental. Jesus said, "Blessed are the merciful, for they will be shown mercy."[13] And, mercy, said his brother James, "triumphs over judgment."[14]

In most communities, however, a pecking order is firmly in place, sometimes overt and sometimes hidden just below the surface. To be sure, the pitfalls of judgmentalism and social ranking were present in our community too. But their presence was minimal and, in many ways, self-correcting. In other words, the community had a shared impulse to push these tendencies to the side in favor of a higher goal.

I like to describe our friend and Anglican priest Bill Haley as having a collar on one end and a tattoo on the other, because he often dons his clerical collar while wearing flip-flops, exposing a tattoo on his ankle. A decade or more ago Bill set out to form a new community in Washington DC called St. Brendan's in the City. In the early days we met in a rescue mission at the intersection of Fourteenth and R Streets. Our community was small. We sat together in a circle, and our gathering was augmented by candles, a portable altar, and an out-of-tune piano that required our worship leader, Roy, to play different notes in certain keys to create a melody. We passed the communion cup around a circle of friends, which included the student struggling to survive grad school, the World Bank staffer trying to change global economics, and the man from the rescue mission who'd been detoxing for a week or more. I'll never forget receiving the communion cup one Sunday night—given the context, it was filled with grape juice, not wine—from a man to my right. He was perhaps fifty years old, a recent immigrant with a thick accent, suffering eyes, and a kind smile. "The blood of Christ . . . shed for you," he said slowly, referencing the symbolism of the Eucharist, as he carefully passed the cup while doing his best to steady his shaking hands. He was a guest at the rescue mission, presumably recovering from a life of alcoholism. But on that day he became my brother.

When I was growing up, the Eucharist was always a holy event, one I still miss when I attend services that don't feature communion as a central part of the worship service. Over the years I've rediscovered the Eucharist as an event that is not just holy but also earthy. Frederick Buechner still surprises me with his breathtaking interpretation of the phenomenon he refers to as simply "Holy Communion":

> When feeding at this implausible table, Christians believe that they are communing with the Holy One himself, his spirit enlivening their spirits, heating the blood, and gladdening the heart just the way wine, as spirits, can.
>
> They are also, of course, communing with each other. To eat any meal together is to meet at the level of our most basic need. It is hard to preserve your dignity with butter on your chin, or to keep your distance when asking for the tomato ketchup.
>
> To eat this particular meal together is to meet at the level of our most basic humanness, which involves our need not just for food but for each other. I need you to help fill my emptiness just as you need me to help fill yours. As for the emptiness that's still left over, well, we're in it together, or it in us. Maybe it's most of what makes us human and makes us brothers and sisters.
>
> The next time you walk down the street, take a good look at every face you pass and in your mind say, "Christ died for thee." . . . That slob. That phony. That crook. That saint. That damned fool. *Christ* died for thee. Take and eat this in remembrance that Christ died for *thee*.[15]

Yes, yes, and yes! Sometimes symbol and ceremony, the Eucharist in this case, help us live into our calling to love one another better than any sermon, song, or shred of advice. It's intriguing that Jesus told us to do so few things to remember him. Communion was one.

But what was it about our experiences on a hospital ship sailing the world or in a fledgling church in DC that fostered communities that were less likely to judge and, therefore, more prone to love?

FROM HOSTILITY TO HOSPITALITY

We know we live in a world that is increasingly afraid. When we are afraid, we tend to pull away, isolate ourselves, and sometimes nurture suspicion. We justify this behavior under the guise of protection. But our souls crave communities where we can trust, discover, and contribute. We long to give away ourselves to one another, yet we are often unaware of this fundamental need. So we live in a great tension between what we fear and what we love.

Writing almost two decades ago, Henri Nouwen described an essential movement of faith: from hostility to hospitality. Our vocation, he wrote, is "to convert the *hostis* into a *hospes,* the enemy into a guest and to create the free and fearless space where [community] can be formed and fully experienced."[16]

Admittedly, Nouwen's language feels lofty, even utopian, in an increasingly messy world replete with terrorism, crime, and other forms of violence, all with the power to incite fear. But for all Nouwen's idealism, he presents a very practical approach. Hospitality, according to Nouwen's understanding of several biblical texts, is not merely "soft sweet kindness, tea parties, bland conversations and a general atmosphere of coziness,"[17] but rather a muscular virtue with the capability of disarming enemies, healing age-old rifts, and overcoming violence. In essence, hospitality creates space where a stranger can enter and become a friend instead of an enemy.

Hospitality shouldn't be reserved only for the stranger but should be offered in any relationship, or potential relationship, where both the host and guest can experience transforming change, the kind of change that produces genuine friendship.

Hospitality is hard work, however, because it requires us to create space for one another. According to Nouwen, we must pursue a kind of "poverty of the mind," a setting aside of opinions, assumptions, and judgments in order to understand another's perspective. Hospitality also requires a "poverty of the heart," a setting aside of worries, jealousies, and prejudices.[18]

I realize all this may feel like dangerous ground. Aren't we meant to carefully discern truth and pursue it with faith? Isn't there virtue in guarding and protecting what we believe? If we set aside our convictions, even for a moment, don't we open ourselves up to potentially dangerous ideas?

These are important questions, honest ones, worthy of discussion. In creating space for another, we do not need to give up our convictions. In fact, sometimes encountering another's perspective serves to affirm our own. When I lived in West Africa, I often discussed faith with Muslim friends. I spent a good deal of that time understanding their story, their beliefs, and their dreams. I listened a lot, seeking to understand their way of life. Sometimes they would shift their position regarding faith or their perspective on Jesus or even Christianity. Often we would conclude our time with prayer.

Through these experiences I discovered that a genuine understanding of another's perspective can lead to personal change even as both remain committed to their own convictions. At a minimum we usually leave such encounters with greater empathy. For the most part my convictions deepened through these experiences; they didn't substantially shift. If anything, my Muslim friends' commitment and perseverance challenged my own faith even as I remained convinced that Jesus is "the way and the truth and the life."[19]

But sometimes our convictions do need to change. Bringing preconceived notions to a conversation can make it impossible to genuinely consider the other person, let alone that person's perspective. Encountering a perspective that confronts our assumptions can help us consider where we might be wrong. Throughout history major changes often began when cataclysmic events forced people to reconsider what they had assumed to be true. Even in relatively recent times, we have witnessed what happens when whole swaths of God-fearing people defend racism, slavery, or misogyny. Those perspectives had to be confronted, and that may have brought fear or uncertainty to those with deeply held convictions even though they were wrong. Slavery in the British empire and apartheid in South Africa are but two examples. The resulting turmoil ushered in changes of perspective, not to mention needed repentance and restitution. Similarly, at a personal level the hardest experiences of life—suffering, loss, or sudden change—often have the greatest potential to significantly shift our perspective.

But there is also a more basic question to consider. What are we afraid of, really afraid of? If our convictions—whether theological or practical—are true, will they not stand the test of time and remain unchanged regardless of our personal ability to defend them? After all, the Author of truth doesn't need our help in defending that which will remain for all eternity. God is not afraid; we don't need to be afraid either. Rather, God gently invites us to join him in personifying truth—that is, in living truth in love—not just intellectually defending what we deem to be true. Our highest calling is not to be right but rather to become righteous and just. Above all, God desires that we become like him—patient, humble, and loving, in addition to being truthful. I have both seen and experienced that God will often dislodge some unquestioned conviction in us in order to humble us and reawaken us to love. Pride, especially intellectual pride, which is often disguised as theological correctness, dexterity at apologetics, or biblical expertise can be the greatest barrier to loving God and others. God is as concerned about who we are becoming as about what we believe. The God of love will not let us slip down some slippery slope of deception because we have the intellectual humility to listen to the stories, aspirations, and, yes, beliefs of others. When we personify love in this way, we will be surprised by the power of God in our midst.

IMPOSSIBLE UNTIL DONE

Becoming a community of differents, like the third race of the early church, seems impossible for many. If you've participated in a multicultural community or sought out conversations with people significantly different from yourself, you understand it's hard work. Sometimes years of investment in hospitality bring only grief. It can kick the idealism out of the most well-intentioned altruist.

Yet Jesus offers an astonishing invitation. Unfortunately, it's rarely talked about, maybe because it's scary or prone to misinterpretation. Or maybe we simply assume people know about it, though few seem to understand and experience it.

The invitation? To exchange your life with Christ's and to live out his power and presence here on earth through your thoughts, emotions, words, and deeds. The apostle Paul summarized it with a profound statement: "I no longer live, but Christ lives in me."[20] Theologians call it *theosis,* an oft-misunderstood word that simply means participation in the life of God. When we tap into this idea, even momentarily, everything changes. Our motives change; our perspective shifts; we change. As a result, we begin to want to reach out to people who are different from us. Our fear dissipates; we no longer fear losing what we've "attained." We experience a love for others that surprises us, not to mention those around us.

The key to living this way? Letting our fear drive us to a place of desperation. So often we do all we can to push fear away or ignore it altogether. We esteem the person who appears to have it all together. His emotions are controlled. She refrains from comment. He defers to others. But sometimes this person is simply afraid—afraid of displaying emotion or of saying the wrong thing. Being brave requires us to muster the courage to feel deeply. Our emotions can drive us toward honest reflection, decision, and, ultimately, action. In this sense fear can be a gift, but only if we are honest with ourselves.

It's in this place of desperation where the Spirit of God meets us most intensely. "Come to me, all you who are weary and burdened, and I will give you rest," said Jesus.[21] Yet the empowering presence of God, the participation in the life of God through his Holy Spirit, remains elusive for so many followers of Jesus. It's this very promise—the sending of the Holy Spirit by the Father[22]—however, that more than anything can help us live a life of authentic faith. Without the Spirit of God consuming our hearts, inspiring our thoughts, and coursing through our veins, following Jesus becomes an exercise in futility. Ironically, while God sends his Spirit to help us overcome fear, many people are afraid of his Spirit, some deathly afraid. His answer? "Trust in God, and trust also in me."[23] I encourage you to simply ask him to come into your life in a new way.

God answers desperate prayers.

Jesus said, "Blessed are those who hunger and thirst . . . for they will be filled."[24] God designed the universe in such a way that desperation—that commitment of trust and the associated feeling of being utterly undone—is a powerful gateway to change. It can lead to the *metanoia,* the complete change of heart, or repentance, that John the Baptist talked about. It can open your heart to an increased filling of the power of God. And it can inform prayers that invite an entirely new direction for your life.

Consider this desperate prayer from John Wesley:

I am no longer my own but yours.
Put me to what you will
rank me with whom you will;
put me to doing,
put me to suffering;
let me be employed for you,
or laid aside for you,
exalted for you,
or brought low for you;
let me be full,

let me be empty,
let me have all things,
let me have nothing:
I freely and wholeheartedly yield all things
to your pleasure and disposal.
And now, glorious and blessed God,
Father, Son and Holy Spirit,
you are mine and I am yours. So be it.
And the covenant now made on earth, let it be ratified
    in heaven.[25]

Converting our fears into faith is the business of God. But he's not interested in a gnostic faith, a faith disembodied from the earthiness of day-to-day living. Instead, God desires a faith that engages our emotions and volition as much as our intellect, a faith that shocks those around us because our words or actions, although occurring in the natural world, have their origin in the divine.

The life of Christ expressing itself through our feeble limbs, frail words, and fragile actions is a powerful thing. It is strong enough to correct the course of a fallen world and bold enough to transform our faith in the process.

As you surrender your fear for faith, be forewarned, however. Some may call you strange, even peculiar. But as my teenage sons say, "Don't worry, Dad. Awkward is the new cool!"

Six

Break Open the Sky

We need, in love, to practice only this: letting
each other go. For holding on comes easily; we
do not need to learn it.

—Rainer Maria Rilke

S ometimes compassion separates the world into two groups of
people: the haves and the have-nots, the benefactors and the ben-
eficiaries, the heroes and the victims, us and them. When the world is
divided in this way, our faith limps.

But it doesn't have to be this way.

One of our closest African friends is a man named Cyprien. A
Rwandan but born in Congo, Cyprien has lived a life that only those
who know him fully appreciate. As a young shepherd boy, he sneaked
into a local school because he was hungry to learn. In 1994 he risked
his life to help victims of the genocide in Rwanda. Today he is design-
ing peace-building programs in Pakistan. Cyprien is wise; he's been a

mentor to both Belinda and me. He is humble, still referring to himself as a villager despite his master's degree. And he is full of life; his Morgan Freeman–voice booms with laughter and joy.

Always the teacher, when Cyprien stands before people in rural Rwanda or Congo, he asks them what they can do to overcome poverty or conflict in their village. Invariably, with dropped shoulders and downcast eyes, they say, "We can do nothing; we are vulnerable; we are poor." They refer to the foreigners, "the white man," who must bring them help.

Cyprien challenges them. "My brothers and sisters," he says, "do you have hands?"

"Yes, we have hands!" they say.

"Then show me your hands!" Cyprien implores. They lift their hands, mimicking Cyprien, waving them in the air with increasing enthusiasm.

Cyprien continues, "Do you have feet?"

"Yes, we have feet!" they reply.

"Then show me your feet!" They raise their feet from the ground, stomping them playfully. Smiles begin to break into laughter. Conversations ripple across the room as people ask one another what this man is saying to them.

"Do you have people in your village who are more vulnerable than you?" Cyprien asks. Slowly individuals begin to identify a widow without food, a father without a job, a family without a livable home. "Then, my friends, what can we do together to help those people?"

Within weeks the villagers create a plan to build a house, provide means for a widow to earn income, or help families take in an orphan.

All this is done without charity from outside the community.

UNCHARITABLE

The word *charity* means something far different today than in previous times. In the Latin version of the Bible, the Vulgate, the word was used to express the highest form of love, *agape* in Greek, meaning selfless devotion to another. Today *charity* means giving aid—usually financial assistance, food, or maybe clothes—to those in need. But too often those who receive charity feel pitied rather than loved.

Several years ago while I was teaching a class on microfinance, a man from Ghana openly, and rightly, challenged my use of the word *help*. In frustration he told me that Africa doesn't need more pity from the West. Another African friend described the subservient relationship charity can foster by saying, "A hand open is always a hand under," meaning the one who receives generally feels inferior.

To be sure, financial assistance is sometimes needed. Crises such as an earthquake, fire, hurricane, or sudden war may require an urgent, charitable response. But far too often the mind-set, ethics, and delivery mechanisms that accompany charity are unnecessary and unwelcome. As a result, problems are often made worse rather than better.

We've heard this before, right? Some of us have immersed ourselves in *When Helping Hurts* by Steve Corbett and Brian Fikkert or Robert Lupton's *Toxic Charity*. We understand it is important that we "do no harm" when attempting to genuinely love our neighbors. Yet even though we've made strides in this area, the enterprise of charity forcefully carries on with all its ill effects. Well-intended but detrimental efforts still dominate the philanthropic landscape. Recipients of these efforts still feel like second-class persons. Pity still pervades our efforts at making the world a better place.

In an article published by ONE, the author and activist Emily Roenigk refers to the dark side of pity-based charity as "poverty porn" and explains that such charity empowers the wrong person:

> Poverty porn tells donors that because of their position in society and because of their resources they have the ability to be the saviors in vulnerable communities they might know nothing about. It fails to awaken Western audiences to the mutual need for transformation they share with their poor brothers and sisters and instead perpetuates dangerous paternalism. . . . Poverty porn objectifies its subjects, defining them by their suffering and stripping them of the vital components of all human life—agency, autonomy and unlimited potential. Advertisements and marketing materials depicting the suffering of the poor and soliciting financial support may inadvertently tell subjects that they are indeed helpless beneficiaries, dependent on the support of the wealthy for any lasting transformation.[1]

Decades of charity, with its implicit savior-victim narrative, have reduced our understanding of poverty to something far too simple. Some have exploited the suffering of others to gain attention for themselves and their efforts. As a result we are numb to the great issues we face today.

Even worse than desensitization is the false identity charity fosters for both the donor and the victim. These false identities can be harmful, even dangerous. The victim identity can stay with the receiver long after the crisis is over, shaping the person's self-perception for a lifetime, even affecting generations to come. The savior identity can be addicting. It creates a false expression of faith and can permeate the soul of a community, social class, or nation.

Seeing people *as people*—not as "the poor," "victims," or mere objects of compassion—can turn the conventional idea of charity upside down. The people closest to the problems have the highest potential for changing their own communities, neighborhoods, and families. Inviting them *into* the problem and empowering them toward solutions makes all the difference. And once we encounter and experience *their* joy in influencing their world, there is no going back to old ways.[2]

But understanding the vagaries of charity is not enough. We must go deeper into ourselves as well, into the heart and soul of who we are, and discover what we really believe.

CHICKEN-COOP COUNSEL

In the kitchen of our house sits a red-headed wooden rooster we've affectionately named Ned. Ned sits alongside Curly, a ceramic pig, but that's another story for another time. Ned is only eighteen inches tall, with limbs attached by wire, allowing us to position him in various poses just for fun. Because Ned is in our kitchen, where we spend a lot of time, his fiery coiffure and endearing sneer are an ever-present fixture in our family.

When we talk about Ned, we are sometimes reminded of the pecking order. I've referred to it several times already, but if you don't know what that is, don't worry; surely you've experienced it. Originally it was used to describe the way in which chickens maintain their dominance over one another by literally pecking other chickens with their beaks, but the term has become a descriptor of any informal hierarchical social system. If you're still not sure what I am talking about, stand back and observe a group of people interacting—any group of any age in any situation will do. You will see the pecking order at work almost immediately. "I love your dress!" "How was your trip to Europe?" "Did you see the game?" Behind the comments, questions, and quips is a subtle ordering of who's more important, more knowledgeable, better looking, more traveled, and so on. The more insecure a person is within the group, the more likely it is that person will attempt to determine his or her importance, often unconsciously, according to a subjective hierarchy, which is usually set by the most dominant member of the group.

None of us is immune to this. We experience pecking orders all the time at school, the office, home, and even church. Advertising campaigns depend on the pecking order. Social clubs thrive on it. The world of sports depends on it. Colleges lead with it. You can observe it in the way rich and famous people jockey for position by keeping up with the social expectations set by Hollywood, Nashville, or New York. Unfortunately, too many people determine their worth according to the pecking order.

Pecking orders exist in the humbler corners of society as well. In *Behind the Beautiful Forevers: Life, Death, and Hope in a Mumbai Undercity,* Katherine Boo describes the pecking order in a slum by saying, "What was unfolding in Mumbai was unfolding elsewhere, too." She wrote:

> In the age of global market capitalism, hopes and grievances
> were narrowly conceived, which blunted a sense of common
> predicament. Poor people didn't unite; they competed fero-

ciously amongst themselves for gains as slender as they were provisional. And this undercity strife created only the faintest ripple in the fabric of the society at large. The gates of the rich, occasionally rattled, remained unbreached. The politicians held forth on the middle class. The poor took down one another, and the world's great, unequal cities soldiered on in relative peace.[3]

In the world of charity, the pecking order is also very much alive and well. The very idea of charity establishes a pecking order of haves and have-nots. Too often we give or get involved in social causes in order to feel better about ourselves. When we do, social justice, philanthropy, and ministry become part of the pecking order.

There are benefits to escaping the tyranny of the pecking order, even for chickens. In her 2015 TED Talk, Margaret Heffernan discussed the benefits of teamwork by highlighting a study involving chickens:

> An evolutionary biologist at Purdue University named William Muir studied chickens. He was interested in productivity—I think it's something that concerns all of us—but it's easy to measure in chickens because you just count the eggs. He wanted to know what could make his chickens more productive, so he devised a beautiful experiment. Chickens live in groups, so first of all, he selected just an average flock, and he let it alone for six generations. But then he created a second group of the individually most productive chickens—you could call them super-chickens—and he put them together in a superflock, and each generation, he selected only the most productive for breeding.

After six generations had passed, what did he find? Well, the first group, the average group, was doing just fine. They were all plump and fully feathered and egg production had increased dramatically. What about the second group? Well, all but three were dead. They'd pecked the rest to death.[4]

For both chickens and humans, sometimes the pecking order doesn't end well.

Despite this scientific evidence, it's not easy to overcome our relentless tendency to compare and compete. The pecking order is deeply ingrained in all of us. How do we, in fact, liberate ourselves from our propensity to find identity through comparison? I believe if we can break free from the fear that keeps us trapped in this pervasive malaise, we will experience nothing short of a revolution, a breakthrough on a seismic scale. Liberating ourselves from the pecking order doesn't only redeem our day-to-day experiences and our charitable engagement; it also redeems our faith. Life without the pecking order is radical indeed.

But how can we be free?

THE GREAT ESCAPE

When Jesus paraded the unlikely characters in his Great Sermon—the poor, the meek, the mourners, the merciful, and so on—he wasn't only elevating certain virtues or values. He was also presenting an entirely different way of life by overturning the prevailing system of meritocracy. Jesus was proposing something altogether different, something radical—so radical it got him killed. He was offering a way to escape the pecking order.

In order to escape the pecking order, we need a new way to determine how we value human life. When Jesus said, "Blessed are those who hunger and thirst for righteousness, for they will be filled," he presented a capstone principle for living. We usually interpret *righteousness—dikaiosune* in Greek—as personal virtue, but when Jesus used this term, he was speaking of much more. The Old Testament word for righteousness[5] means deliverance or salvation, referring to God's putting right that which is wrong.[6] This definition includes both the action of God (his relationship with his people) and the conduct of his people (their relationships with one another). This should be no surprise, given the quintessential tenet of Jewish life, the Shema, which begins, "Hear, O Israel: The LORD our God, the LORD is one. Love the LORD your God with all your heart and with all your soul and with all your strength."[7] Jesus added the second great commandment, "Love your neighbor as yourself,"[8] when responding to a lawyer's question:

> "Teacher, which is the greatest commandment in the Law?"
>
> Jesus replied, " 'Love the Lord your God with all your heart and with all your soul and with all your mind.' This is the first and greatest commandment. And the second is like it: 'Love your neighbor as yourself.' All the Law and the Prophets hang on these two commandments."[9]

The apostle Paul followed Jesus by saying that "the entire law is fulfilled in keeping this one command: 'Love your neighbor as yourself.' "[10] This understanding of righteousness sheds fascinating light on the meaning of Jesus's sermon. His logic was controversial and radical, to be sure, but also impeccable. Let me summarize:

1. You cannot live the life God intended by keeping to a set of dos and don'ts (Matthew 5:20, reinforced by Paul in Ephesians 2:8).
2. Only those who hunger and thirst for righteousness will experience the life God intended (Matthew 5:6).
3. Hungering and thirsting for righteousness requires a right relationship with God and each other (Matthew 22:40).
4. Right relationships are given and empowered by God and characterized by love (John 13:35).
5. In the end only love fulfills the law (Matthew 23:23, Luke 10:30–37).

Here's another way to think about the dilemma we all face:

- Everyone falls prey to the pecking order.
- Jesus offers a way out.
- Love is the elegant answer.

But if it is this simple, why do we experience the pecking order almost every day of our lives? Why so much insecurity?

I suggest we don't really understand love. God's love is unconditional, undeserved, relentless, and unending. It is the basis for our value, our essence, our being. What we do—whether good, mediocre, or bad—doesn't change his love for us. We cannot be more loved by God; we cannot be loved less either.

If we grasp this kind of supreme love, who needs a pecking order?

Grasping this kind of love in order to live beyond the pecking order is no easy feat.

But it *is* possible.

And it's been possible for a long time.

STRIKING UP A CONVERSATION (WITH GOD)

Nicolas Herman was born in 1614 in a region known as Lorraine in modern-day France. He joined the army for food and a stipend—his family were peasants—and fought in the Thirty Years' War. An injury brought him home, however.[11] After a stint as a hermit and then as a footman, he entered a Carmelite monastery in Paris as a lay brother because he didn't have the education to become a priest. "Plagued by a limp," and referring to himself as "a great awkward fellow who broke everything,"[12] Herman worked for more than fifty years as a kitchen aid and an in-house cobbler. He cooked meals, slopped food, scrubbed pots, and mended shoes.[13]

When Herman joined the Carmelites, he took the name "Lawrence of the Resurrection," but he was more commonly known as Brother Lawrence by his fellow monks. If it weren't for a short essay titled simply "Maxims," sixteen letters to friends, and a handful of recorded conversations, his life would have been lost to history.

Googling "Brother Lawrence" today draws several million hits.

For Lawrence, everyday life, or "common business" as he called it, was the means through which we come to know God. He believed it *wasn't* necessary to "have great things to do. . . . We can do little things for God," he said.[14]

> I turn the cake that is frying on the pan for love of Him, and
> that done, if there is nothing else to call me, I prostrate my-
> self in worship before Him, who has given me grace to work;
> afterwards I rise happier than a king. It is enough for me to pick
> up but a straw from the ground for the love of God.[15]

Lawrence lived "as if there were no one save God and me in the world." He "insisted that, to be constantly aware of God's presence, it is necessary to form the habit of continually talking with Him throughout each day."[16] Isolated, but not cloistered, Lawrence became known for his peaceful presence and practical wisdom. He died in relative obscurity in 1691. But his essay, letters, and conversations became the basis for a small book called *The Practice of the Presence of God.*

Lawrence's antidote to the pecking order is simple yet profound. We can know love through a conversational relationship with God. But what I like most about his work is that it feels possible, doable, livable. If he could experience God in this way, he believed others, and not just clerics or monks, could too:

> There is not in the world a kind of life more sweet and delightful than that of a continual conversation with God. Those only can comprehend it who practice and experience it; yet I do not advise you to do it from that motive. It is not pleasure which we ought to seek in this exercise; but let us do it from a principle of love, and because God would have us.[17]

Saints and scholars throughout the centuries have referenced Lawrence. Wesley commended him. A. W. Tozer recommended him. Frank Laubach titled a book after him. And Dallas Willard, one of the most sought-after philosophers and theologians of our day, waxed eloquently about Brother Lawrence's influence: "Today I continue to believe that people are meant to live in an ongoing conversation with God, speaking and being spoken to."[18] Willard wrote:

> Our relationship with God is not a consumerist relationship;
> nor do Christians understand their faith to be a consumer
> religion. . . . We are participants, not spectators. Accordingly,
> we seek to interact with God in a relationship of listening and
> speaking.[19]

If the idea of hearing God is new, strange, or even threatening somehow, you are in good company. *Newsweek* once ran an article about prayer, originally titled, "Talking to God," which quoted several studies on the practice of prayer in the United States. It pointed out that nearly 80 percent of all Americans prayed at least once a week, with more than half (57 percent) reporting praying at least once a day. According to the article, even atheists and agnostics prayed, nearly one in five daily.[20] More recent data by sociologist Rodney Stark confirms this data.[21]

While *talking to God* is broadly practiced, *hearing from God* is not. And those who "experience a directing word from God rarely speak about it."[22] Why? Because they are afraid what others will think of them.

To be sure, hearing God is a delicate area, rife with subjectivity and some modest theological controversy. Yet I believe Willard is right: *we are meant to hear from God.* God wants to talk to us because he loves us. Hearing from God breaks the temptation to live in response to the thousands of voices we hear every day.

If you are willing to accept the invitation, Willard's book *Hearing God* is an invaluable guide, whether you are new to the idea of hearing God speak or a veteran. Willard provides a solid theological framework, a strong biblical basis, and helpful practical guidance. I highly recommend it.

As we begin to experience the love of God in the form of a conversational relationship, we no longer feel the pull of the pecking order. Affirmation from God supplants our misunderstood need to constantly check in with others, hoping to feel better about ourselves. When the God of all galaxies, the Author of truth, the Architect of love, and the only Audience in the universe that matters tells us *he* loves us, what more do we need?

Thankfully, as sublime as it is, this supreme love is not left undefined. The apostle Paul shows us how the "most excellent way" plays out in real life:

> If I speak in the tongues of men or of angels, but do not have love, I am only a resounding gong or a clanging cymbal. If I have the gift of prophecy and can fathom all mysteries and all knowledge, and if I have a faith that can move mountains, but do not have love, I am nothing. If I give all I possess to the poor and give over my body to hardship that I may boast, but do not have love, I gain nothing.
>
> Love is patient, love is kind. It does not envy, it does not boast, it is not proud. It does not dishonor others, it is not self-seeking, it is not easily angered, it keeps no record of wrongs. Love does not delight in evil but rejoices with the truth. It always protects, always trusts, always hopes, always perseveres.
>
> Love never fails. But where there are prophecies, they will cease; where there are tongues, they will be stilled; where there is knowledge, it will pass away. For we know in part and we

prophesy in part, but when completeness comes, what is in part disappears. When I was a child, I talked like a child, I thought like a child, I reasoned like a child. When I became a man, I put the ways of childhood behind me. For now we see only a reflection as in a mirror; then we shall see face to face. Now I know in part; then I shall know fully, even as I am fully known.

And now these three remain: faith, hope and love. But the greatest of these is love.[23]

FAMILY, EVEN

When it comes to love, either "everybody counts or nobody counts."[24] I think Jesus would agree.

In recent years the idea of justice has been, in a sense, rediscovered by the likes of Nicholas Wolterstorff, Walter Brueggemann, and Timothy Keller. Justice, it turns out, is closely related to the biblical concept of righteousness; the two ideas are inseparable, in fact.[25] Like righteousness, justice is concerned about right relationships, and it is closely connected to the ethic of love.

Some time ago I was trying to explain the concept of justice to a group of people who were struggling to think about justice in relational terms. For so long we have considered justice in mostly legal terms, focusing exclusively on repairing what was broken. Both these elements are included in the biblical idea of justice, but they fall short of capturing its fullness.

I reached out to a friend, Micah Bournes, for help. Micah is a spoken-word artist, musician, and hip-hop theologian. We talked about how people think about justice, the recent recovery of the biblical ideal, and the surge in activism among certain demographics. I also explained my dilemma in trying to communicate the broader definition of justice.

A few weeks later Micah sent me a piece called "Is Justice Worth It?" We convinced my colleagues at World Relief and the Justice Conference to invest in bringing Micah's words to life. Micah worked with a team in Portland called Epipheo to put animation to his words. Micah's "Is Justice Worth It?" may be the most impactful video in World Relief's history, and it has become the most-watched video Micah has ever produced.

The video is compelling for several reasons. It's personal, emotional, and theological, and it conveys the urgency of justice. Most powerful to me is the way it explains the essence of justice in relational terms and provides the key for escaping the vagaries of charity.

Here is the text, and you can also view the video:

> A lot of people see justice as the most futile thing you
>   can do with your life.
> Give your life completely to business and you see the
>   money piling up.
> Be a health nut, eat right, go to the gym,
> And your muscles will grow and your body will look
>   good
> And you'll see results.
> But when it comes to justice, it seems like you just can't
>   get ahead;
> You patch up one hole and something else rips open;

You bring peace to one region and war breaks out in
    another;
You rebuild after an earthquake and a tsunami hits;
And you work and you work and you work and there's
    never any profit;
There's no bank where you can store a surplus amount
    of justice in.
Stability is never permanent.
Something always tips and people always ask
Is it even worth it?
And that question, though understandable, it's—
I mean, quite frankly, it's ridiculous.
And it rarely comes from those who are actually tired
    from pursuing justice
And not just tired of the idea;
It rarely comes from people who've labored for years
And have good reason to ask it.
And you know why they never ask?
Those type of people become friends with those
    who suffer—
Family even.
Because it's one thing to wonder if someone else's
    freedom is worth fighting for
But when you begin to identify with that someone
    else—
Commune with them—
That's when the question is no longer worth asking.

That's when it becomes offensive even.

What do you mean, "Is it worth my time?"

That doesn't even deserve an answer;

I don't care how long it takes!

I don't care how many times we fail!

I don't care how little progress is made . . .

You never stop fighting for your own.[26]

When we define the problems of the world in terms of people—real people who belong to each other—everything changes. No longer is justice only about repairing what's broken; it's also about "fighting for your own." When we reframe righteousness and justice as relational in nature, the rules change. The expectations and patterns of family or friendship now apply. Unlike charity, friendship is mutual. Both parties give and both receive. Friendship is transformational, not merely transactional. It requires commitment, not merely a one-off interaction. Above all, the motive that drives the friendship and holds it together is love. Love is fierce, stronger than activism, justice, or even righteousness. It contains the power to sustain our commitment well beyond the problems, successes, and even failures.

Jesus said, "Blessed are the pure in heart, for they will see God."[27] Søren Kierkegaard interpreted purity of heart as willing "one thing," saying, "In truth, to will one thing, then, can only mean to will the Good."[28] When we hunger and thirst for the one thing, for God himself, laying down our agenda and repenting, if necessary, for our duplicity, we experience his love in new ways. And only when we begin to know—*really know*—God's love, can we genuinely love one another.

John beautifully distills the essence of this principle in his first letter to the early church:

> Dear friends, since God so loved us, we also ought to love one
> another. No one has ever seen God; but if we love one another,
> God lives in us and his love is made complete in us.
>
> This is how we know that we live in him and he in us:
> He has given us of his Spirit. And we have seen and testify
> that the Father has sent his Son to be the Savior of the world.
> If anyone acknowledges that Jesus is the Son of God, God
> lives in them and they in God. And so we know and rely on
> the love God has for us.
>
> God is love. Whoever lives in love lives in God, and God in
> them.[29]

Then John concludes his discourse with a powerful crescendo: he pronounces the end of fear for those who love:

> There is no fear in love. But perfect love drives out fear, because
> fear has to do with punishment. The one who fears is not made
> perfect in love.
>
> We love because he first loved us.[30]

FREE TO BE FREE

I want to experience this kind of love every day, but so often I don't know where to start. Without a full and ongoing immersion in such love, I slip back into the pecking-order mind-set.

You too?

Pursuing love for ourselves sounds selfish, doesn't it? But receiving love requires me to admit that I am dependent, needy, even desperate, that I have a deficit I cannot fill on my own. In my worst moments I still try to fill that void by doing good, which for me is tantamount to supplying my own needs on the backs of people I deem less fortunate than I. Augustine said, "Our hearts are restless until they find rest in you."[31] Resting in God requires a measure of honesty and vulnerability seldom found in cowboy activists like me.

In order to genuinely serve others, especially the most vulnerable, we must first admit our own vulnerability.[32] We need to grasp the unfathomable love of God lavished upon us despite our glories, our regrets, and our failures. We need to saturate our souls in grace, plunging our shame, our dreams, our hopes, and our insecurities into the depths of an acceptance not conditioned upon merit or performance. In that still, sometimes barren place, we need to listen to what God wants to say to us:

"I love you . . ."
"You are forgiven . . ."
"You belong to me . . ."
"I am yours . . ."

When we receive love from God, the ground on which we stand suddenly becomes level. Now we can freely give. "It is for freedom that Christ has set us free," said Paul.[33]

With our liberation comes another liberation: that of the people we genuinely want to help. By redefining the playing field as level, by considering them friends, we invite the outsiders inside. They become part of the family, no longer excluded because of color, status, economy, language, or geography. They become us and we, them. Mother Teresa said, "If we have no peace, it is because we have forgotten that we belong to each other."[34] The apostle Paul said, "If one part suffers, every part suffers with it."[35] Shifting our perspective from us and them to brother, sister, friend, and family is foundational to a life characterized by authentic faith. With that shift, those who suffer are better empowered to solve the problems *they* face, even as we consider their example in the problems *we* face.

Think of the potential that comes with liberating our friends from being bystanders in their own suffering to being actors in bringing solutions. Consider the nearly one billion people who struggle with hunger,[36] the nearly eight hundred million people who live on less than two dollars a day,[37] the eleven million undocumented immigrants in the United States,[38] the twenty-seven million slaves in the world.[39] What would come of the world if we began to see a step change in how these friends engaged their problems?

When our identity is based in scarcity rather than love, we impose dangerous categories, which become the basis for the pecking order. We compare ourselves to one another, defining our worth falsely, often at the expense of someone else. When, instead, we anchor our identity in love and in the abundance that accompanies it, we no longer need categories by which to define or compare ourselves. We are free to celebrate with others when they succeed and to empathize with them when they don't. We are free to release others rather than try to hold them back.

Several years ago *New York Times* journalists Nicholas Kristof and Sheryl WuDunn wrote a book called *Half the Sky: Turning Oppression into Opportunity for Women Worldwide.*[40] The title comes from a Chinese poem that refers to women comprising half the world's population, or "half the sky." When we consider how many people are living in the shadows merely because of where they were born, their gender, the color of their skin, or the life they inherited, we are talking about billions of people. When we include these brothers, these sisters, these friends as agents, leaders, even trailblazers in their neighborhoods, villages, and communities with the full potential to bring change, and when they recover their God-given dignity along the way and discover their divine purpose in the world, we are talking about a wholesale liberation of more than half the planet. "We are not trapped or locked up in these bones," said Mosley. "No, no, we are free to change," free to be free.

If this isn't breaking open the sky, then what is?

Part 3

RISK

It must be considered that there is nothing more difficult to carry out nor more doubtful of success nor more dangerous to handle than to initiate a new order of things; for the reformer has enemies in all those who profit by the old order, and only lukewarm defenders in all those who would profit by the new order; this lukewarmness arising partly from the incredulity of mankind who does not truly believe in anything new until they actually have experience of it.

—Niccolo Machiavelli

Seven

Learning to Fly

Scared is what you're feeling. Brave is what
you're doing.

—Emma Donoghue

I n the West we like our religion safe.
Some years ago Belinda and I were preparing a team of students for a
trip to Bosnia just after the Dayton Agreement was signed, which ef-
fectively ended the war in the Balkans. We had received permission
from the United Nations to bring aid into the region, including into
Belgrade, then the epicenter of the aggression but also, ironically, a refuge for some. Croatians in particular and some Bosnians too had fled
to Belgrade during the war. A few weeks before our trip, I received a
phone call from the father of one of our students—let's call her Maria—
who was concerned about sending his daughter to Bosnia. I explained
that the war had ended with the peace agreement and told him about
the precautions we were taking. We talked about the fact that his

daughter felt led to express her faith in the context of one of the worst theaters of violence in the latter half of the twentieth century.

In the end Maria chose not to go to Bosnia.

Last year I tried to pull together a group of leaders to join me in South Sudan to visit our brothers and sisters there. The civil war had spread beyond the typical hot spots and was devastating the lives of a considerable number of civilians and jeopardizing their planting season, which put some twelve million people at risk of famine. The South Sudanese were acutely suffering with little support from, or even awareness by, the Western world, including the church. I couldn't escape the urgency of the apostle Paul's words: "If one part suffers, every part suffers with it."[1]

Although we had mapped out a trip that minimized risk, I couldn't deny that the country was at war. People offered a range of reasons for why they couldn't join.

In the end we canceled the trip.

Both Maria and the friends I invited to South Sudan voiced a common concern: they were, understandably, focused more on what they had to give up—a measure of safety—than on what they might gain. For them, the risks were too great. I often make similar choices using the same rationale.

In most of the world, however, risk and faith are not opposing choices. They go hand in hand.

Not long ago I traveled to the Middle East to understand better the Syrian refugee crisis. In Jordan I met the pastor of a church near the Syrian border, in the city of Mafraq. When Pastor Ephraim[2] decided to open his church to Syrian refugee children and their mothers, many of his Jordanian congregants felt they could no longer worship at Ephraim's church. Some left the church for good. Kids from the community taunted the Syrian children as they walked to the church to participate in activities, such as storytelling and art therapy, to overcome their trauma. "They come to us bleeding sometimes," said Ephraim, referring to the cuts, scrapes, and bruises the Syrian children sustained from rocks thrown by local kids. "The message of Jesus is to love our enemies," Ephraim said. "How can we turn them away? We've been trying to reach Syria for nearly fifteen years. Now they are coming to us to ask for help."

Ephraim isn't pursuing a safe religion.

Recently a friend of a friend from Tennessee told me about a trip he took to South Sudan with a group of pastors during another time when South Sudan was experiencing civil war. Most of the local clergy had been killed in the war, so the local Sudanese pled with the visiting team to conduct baptisms in the White Nile. The visitors humbly agreed, only to find that there were more than four hundred people who wished to be baptized. Since my friend was not a pastor, he asked to join the large group of men standing side by side in the river, encircling the pastors and people being baptized. When he approached the men, they vehemently shook their heads and raised their voices, saying, "No, no, no!" while clapping their hands and arms together to demonstrate they were keeping away crocodiles while the pastors baptized their people. It hadn't occurred to these South Sudanese believers that safety—from crocodiles no less—was more important than a public profession of faith.

Taking risks means exposing ourselves to the possibility of danger. For some, risk means the possibility of illness or injury. For others, risk means placing themselves in unknown situations with unfamiliar food or different languages. For many, risk means accepting the possibility of failure.

We regularly take risks when the potential for gain seems to outweigh the potential for loss or harm. "It's worth the risk," we often say, summarizing the risk-reward paradigm that drives our thinking on nearly every level. However, we usually personalize the risk-reward formula, focusing almost exclusively on the potential gain or loss for ourselves rather than for others, let alone for God.

Moreover, risk is often more mundane than we think. When we think of the HIV/AIDS crisis in Africa, we might think about caring for the millions of orphans or serving the mothers taking antiretroviral drugs to prevent mother–to-child transmission. But we don't think about Emmanuel, a gentle, demure African leader who for years traveled the countryside of Rwanda pleading with pastors to care for people living with HIV/AIDS. In the early days of the pandemic, pastors slammed their church doors shut, blaming the victims, labeling the disease a curse from God, and sometimes shaming Emmanuel for asking pastors to care for people living with HIV/AIDS. One pastor even suggested that all such people should be locked in a room together so we "could throw away the key," implying we should let them die.

But Emmanuel pressed on. Months turned into years, and years turned into decades. Slowly the church changed its mind and its theology too. Today Rwanda's pastors are taking the lead in stemming the tide of new infections while serving thousands of people living with HIV/AIDS.

My wife, Belinda, is known for speaking out against violence against women. Last year she climbed Mount Kilimanjaro in Africa with fourteen others to raise awareness and funds for women trapped in the spiral of violence associated with war and conflict zones. Many people consider her an activist who is not afraid to take risks. But most of her time is given to the tedious work of administrating a nonprofit and to the long slog of getting the word out through social and other traditional forms of media to people who have never heard or, worse, really don't care.

Tedious, mundane, and sustained activities matter. Small, often hidden, actions make risk possible. And just like faith, mustard-seed risks can grow up to become the largest trees in the garden.[3]

Faith and risk go hand in hand.

WORTH THE RISK

The God of the universe is prone to taking risks. Consider, for example, his opening act. Creation was a supreme risk. Creating people with free will, all for the sake of love, was an unfathomable risk, one that is impossible to fully comprehend. God, having infinite power, willingly shared power with finite beings so we could join him in bringing shalom. And he took this risk knowing we would betray him. The incarnation was also a huge risk. God dressed in human skin to inaugurate his rescue plan, knowing he would endure rejection, torture, and ultimately death at the hands of those he came to save. Equally risky was the commissioning of a group of ragtag wannabes, us included, to participate with him in bringing change to a broken world, despite myriad anticipated failures.

God is a risk-taker.

And so were the heroes of the Bible. Noah invested a hundred years of his life and his entire reputation in building an ark in the desert.

Abraham left home without a plan for his future, much less a road map to take him there. Moses came out of retirement to face down the leader of an empire in a bid to liberate a fickle would-be nation. Joshua marched around a city in the hope that its walls would somehow fall down before its barbarian inhabitants rallied to defeat him. Daniel risked facing hungry lions to maintain his integrity. David faced a giant from whom everyone else had fled, armed with nothing more than faith and a slingshot. Jeremiah, Ezekiel, Isaiah, Micah, and others took a stand, risking their lives to speak truth to power.

Then there's Jesus, who took staggering risks for "the joy set before him."[4] Just think about the twelve men, who were likely teenagers, that he chose to change the world. Only the team treasurer had a bit of formal training.

Jesus's followers were no less courageous. Consider, for example, the woman of questionable reputation who fearlessly entered the home of Simon the Pharisee.[5] Simon had convened a theological discussion; Jesus was the keynote speaker (although Simon had in mind to scrutinize, not extol, his teaching). The public was invited, provided they sat quietly around the perimeter of the room while the sages held court. Steely eyes would have fastened on the woman as she strode across the room. Imagine her making a beeline for the man who had somehow convinced her she was radically loved, her sins forgiven. She kneeled behind him, assuming the posture of a slave, her lips quivering. Then she began to weep, her tears streaming down her radiant face. Committing a social taboo, she uncovered her head and let her hair spill down upon his feet, mixing with her tears and the dust. She washed his feet clean; she dried them with her hair.

Meanwhile the town gossips whispered, formulating their conjectures, their opinions, their judgments about her relationship with him, and his with her.

Why would this woman risk what little reputation she had left by lavishing such extravagance upon a man she hardly knew? And why would he risk his growing reputation as a holy man by accepting her outrageous public affection?

How audacious. What verve. What . . .

Risk.

Michael Pritzl, front man for a band called The Violet Burning, was so taken by this story that he wrote a song called "The Song of the Harlot" in which he compares his life to the woman in the gospel of Luke who demonstrated extravagant, unashamed worship. "If I could be anyone," Pritzl sings repeatedly as the song builds to a crescendo, and then he fades to the final resolve as he says he would be "the whore at your feet."[6]

Not something you normally hear on Sunday.

THESE ARE THE ONES

I couldn't help noticing the intriguing tattoo on the server at Chipotle during a late-night stop with my son Caleb. On his forearm in large block letters was the word εἰρηνοποιός. I recognized it was Greek but didn't know what it meant. "I like your tattoo," I said. "Tell me what it means."

"It's the Greek word for *peacemaker*," he responded kindly, "from Matthew 5:9." Then he proceeded to quote the verse.

A bit stunned, since I was in the midst of writing this chapter about peacemakers, I babbled embarrassingly, "Um . . . wow . . . um . . .

cool . . . that's really awesome, man!" and awkwardly moved along to pay for my son's chicken burrito.

It turns out the Greek word for *peacemaker* means something far more than someone who merely promotes or instills serenity. It means reconciler, "one who, having received the peace of God in her own heart, brings peace to others," and someone who is concerned "with bringing about a cessation of hostilities."[7] Peacemaking is by no means passive. It involves taking risk. Peacemakers are not afraid to enter the fray in order to establish peace.

When our faith is passive, safe, void of risk, it loses its witness to a world that is increasingly jaded and skeptical. It forfeits its potential to awaken, or reawaken, a dying culture. Safe religion becomes self-absorbed, sentimental, esoteric, or, worse, superstitious.

Having a faith that will not risk means we can only serve when it's safe. South Sudan will have to wait. Yemen too. The families in our inner cities will have to reduce crime on their own. If we remove risk from faith, we cannot send cleanup crews into cities in the wake of riots. It's just too dangerous. It means we'll never buy a meal for a homeless person or staff a shelter for battered women. Something bad might happen.

In his Sermon on the Mount, Jesus announced favor for peacemakers. He promised they would be the "children of God."[8] I grew up in the Midwest, where social conflict is generally avoided at all costs. It's not that our communities were devoid of tension—where there are people, there is tension—but we worked hard, very hard, to avoid even acknowledging there were problems. We often felt this tension in the unsaid word, the absent emotion, and the passive-aggressive tone. Anyone choosing to point a finger at a problem had to be brave enough to upset the apple cart. Cultural norms—whether midwestern or Middle Eastern—that generally favor the status quo become powerful forces for any risk-taker to overcome. Risk requires courage; it's a prerequisite for peacemaking.

Because Jesus was a peacemaker, he was a risk-taker. Jesus was born into conflict, and many hoped he would rise up to become a military Messiah, as David had before him. In fact, the Jews in Jesus's day were ready to take up arms. Just a few decades after Jesus's death, a group of Jews revolted against the Romans.[9]

But Jesus confronted the oppression of his day without violence. His peacemaking was not without risk—costly risk. But rather than fighting violence with violence, Jesus fought violence with vulnerability. He responded to the vice of violence with the virtue of peace—shalom, the intended harmony of God.[10] He never avoided the elephant in the room—whether it was oppression and injustice or the violence that stemmed from sin—but confronted the root causes, embodying the solution in himself. He became a peace offering, bearing the brunt of the world's violence so that peace would triumph.

Peace is expensive. It requires risk-taking. It's personal, and it makes you vulnerable. And peace always involves action. Resistance is part of the calling.

I've met quite a few risk-takers in my day. They are gutsy, not afraid. They enter the fray. And they are not who you might think they are.

Some years ago while working with some peacemaker friends in the Democratic Republic of Congo, I jotted a few stanzas that later became a poem called "These Are the Ones." If you are a peacemaker or aspire to become one, and especially if you are asking whether the cost is worth it, these words are for you:

These are the ones who shout aloud when everyone else
        is silent,
Who slide their hands across their lips when everyone
        screams.
These are the ones who sweep the ash heap of history,
Scouring the scorched earth for signs of hope,
So fragile and frail,
Life so resilient.

These are the ones who fan the feeble flame, who
        incubate,
Who resuscitate dead breath with quivering lips,
Who cup their hands around their becoming,
When green shoots sprout from petrified stump;
When flowers burst from granite crag,
When crowded stars shout their names.

These are the ones who give their lives,
Like the apartheid priest
Who stretched his ebony skin across a white man's
        trembling body
Just as a mob was about to stone.
These are the ones who risk,
Like my friend who saved the other tribe,
Only to be nearly killed for his charity.
These are the ones who love,
Like the woman who forgave the violent man with
        vacant eyes,

The soldier who thieved her life until God stole it back;
Or the refugee who still weeps her loss
Even though she's free.

These are the ones who slip hate letters into bottom
        drawers
And bless the hands that penned them.
These are the ones who sing with different melody,
Who dance to different drum,
Who find each other amidst the cacophony
To draw from mutual wells of wisdom,
Of grace,
Of strength.

These are the ones who stare down impossibility
With tear-stained faces,
Who wage war with vulnerable faith,
Who laugh when devils cry,
Who bolt their sister's hopes to wings that fly.

These are the ones who pray
Without doubt, who shout
Without shrill,
Who grab hold the shoulders of despair
And shake free all vestige of fear.
These are ones who stampede with love,
Who vanquish with humility,
Who overcome through suffering.

These are the ones who fling their dreams against
　　　bright blue sky
Who stitch scarlet thread into rising sun
Who call forth the last to be first
Who usher the least
Into front-row seats.

These are you,
These are me;
These are the ones
Who lament with fury,
Who pray with tempest
Who endure this climb, this race, this fight,
Not with pomp or gold or fist,
But with ostentatious grace and grit.

These are the ones to whom belongs
The promise,
The seven-course meal,
The gaze of heaven,
The hero's dream;
These lovers of God,
These makers of

Peace.

God never promised us safety. Following Jesus means taking risks.
Rest assured: you are in good company. God is a risk-taker too.

JUMP, THEN BUILD YOUR WINGS

When we met Rob Morris, he was living in a small town in rural Texas. He stuck out from the crowd because he was a New Yorker with spiky hair and a love for all things urban. In 2002 Rob traveled to Southeast Asia to discover how he might help end child trafficking. Rob joined up with several undercover investigators from a well-known charity. He was taken to a brothel, where they witnessed children being sold for sex. "We found ourselves standing shoulder to shoulder with predators in a small room," said Rob,

> looking at young girls through a pane of glass. All of the girls wore red dresses with a number pinned to their dress for identification.
>
> They sat, blankly watching cartoons on TV. They were vacant, shells of what a child should be. There was no light in their eyes, no life left. Their light had been taken from them. These children . . . raped each night . . . seven, ten, fifteen times . . . were so young. Thirteen, eleven . . . it was hard to tell. Sorrow covered their faces with nothingness.
>
> Except one girl. One girl who wouldn't watch the cartoons. Her number was 146. She was looking beyond the glass. She was staring out at us with a piercing gaze. There was still fight left in her eyes. There was still life left in this girl. . . .
>
> All of these emotions begin to wreck you. Break you. It is agony. It is aching. It is grief. It is sorrow.[11]

Because this was an undercover investigation, they were unable to rescue the girls that night. The investigators had to collect more evidence in order to free them. When they finally conducted a raid on the brothel, some of the children Rob had seen, including the girl who wore the number 146, were no longer there. To this day Rob does not know what happened. But he will never forget her.

The girl who wore the number 146 changed his life. With a small team Rob moved to New Haven, Connecticut, and launched a non-profit called Love146. He continues to fight modern-day slavery today.

When Rob tells his story, he likes to quote Ray Bradbury, who said sometimes you just have to "jump off the cliff and learn how to make wings on the way down."[12] Taking risks always seems right for other people. Their stories move us, but they don't necessarily compel us to take risks ourselves. The mountains we face are so daunting that we never take the first step. We are afraid—mostly of failure.

But sometimes we need to build our wings in the air.

First steps can be small and practical. Such steps can also be life changing. Rob agreed to travel to Asia. Belinda and I volunteered for a few months. For some, the first step has been picking up a book they thought they could never read. Others watched a TED Talk. All such steps teach us how to fly.

Some years ago I was praying about whether to accept an invitation to do something I really didn't want to do. It was an immense undertaking, a leadership role I knew would be costly. I realized it would involve sacrifice from my family too. The organization was dysfunctional. The board was out of touch, unaware of how bad the situation was. The staff was demoralized; some were outright hostile. A decision to accept this offer would carry an incredible amount of risk.

On May 30 of that year, near the end of a long season of prayer and consideration, Belinda tore a page from the classic devotional *My*

Utmost for His Highest by Oswald Chambers and handed it to me. After a quick glance at the date, I began to read. My heart jumped at the two-word title: "Yes—But . . . !" I wondered if Belinda was second-guessing our decision to decline the offer. Then Chambers's words hit me like a rifle shot, so hard that after reading them I knew I could only say yes to the risk being required of me. The torn page, which contains the words that follow—now underlined, highlighted, and stained with tears—still sits framed in my office:

YES—BUT . . . !
"LORD, I WILL FOLLOW YOU, BUT . . ."

—LUKE 9:61

Suppose God tells you to do something that is an enormous test of your common sense, totally going against it. What will you do? . . . Again and again you will come right up to what Jesus wants, but every time you will turn back at the true point of testing, until you are determined to abandon yourself to God in total surrender. Yet we tend to say, "Yes, but—suppose I do obey God in this matter, what about . . . ?" . . .

. . . If a person is ever going to do anything worthwhile, there will be times when he must risk everything by his leap in the dark. In the spiritual realm, Jesus Christ demands that you risk everything you hold on to or believe through common sense, and leap by faith into what He says. Once you obey, you will immediately find that what He says is as solidly consistent as common sense.

By the test of common sense, Jesus Christ's statements may seem mad, but when you test them by the trial of faith, your findings will fill your spirit with the awesome fact that they are the very words of God. Trust completely in God, and when He brings you to a new opportunity of adventure . . . see that you take it. We act like pagans in a crisis—only one out of an entire crowd is daring enough to invest his faith in the character of God.[13]

Maybe the message in these words will move you too as you contemplate that risk you may need to take.

Are you willing to take a risk? Will you carve an X across the word *but*? When we risk, we love. And where there is love, there is no fear.[14]

Eight

Heretics and Heroes

Show me a hero and I'll write you a tragedy.

—F. Scott Fitzgerald

L yricist Yip Harburg wrote, "All the heroes of tomorrow are the heretics of today."[1]

When you visit Oxford, England, you can't miss the memorial near the center of the city commemorating three sixteenth-century martyrs, including Thomas Cranmer, who compiled *The Book of Common Prayer*. A few blocks away stands prestigious Wycliffe Hall of the University of Oxford, which honors John Wycliffe, a fourteenth-century priest and professor who translated the Bible into the vernacular of the day, Middle English, because he believed everyone should have access to the truth found in sacred Scripture. Wycliffe was declared a heretic in 1415 and his writings banned. In 1428 Pope Martin V had Wycliffe's remains exhumed and burned.[2]

But today he is considered a hero and a saint too.

We could also mention Stephen Biko or Dietrich Bonhoeffer or

Martin Luther King Jr. But heroism isn't limited to martyrs. Living in
Oxford most of his life, C. S. Lewis would have been well versed in the
histories of Wycliffe and Cranmer. Trained in medieval literature,
Lewis felt he was not qualified to speak authoritatively on theology. Yet
most of his major works are distinctly theological and continue to influence mainstream theology today. Lewis discussed controversial ideas
in some of his most popular fictional works, including The Chronicles
of Narnia, in order to avoid being labeled a heretic. Still, he didn't escape criticism altogether.

Even Mother Teresa, who was recently canonized by Pope Francis,
was criticized throughout her life for promoting "a cult of suffering."
Some rejected her as a true follower of Christ.[3]

Today's heroes are fighting causes that are no more popular in our
times than were some of the seminal issues of centuries past. One controversial issue today is forced migration, especially when it involves
resettling refugees in Europe or the United States. When we were "in
our early twenties, my wife, Belinda, and I left our rural hometown in
Wisconsin for what was meant to be a six-month stint in West Africa,
working with Mercy Ships. I took a leave of absence from my career in
business and Belinda from hers as a schoolteacher. Having barely traveled, we were inexperienced and naive. Within months the directors
asked us to colead a medical team among two warring tribes in Northern Ghana. It was here, in the bush, where we first experienced how violence devastates people, often destroying their homes and tearing
families apart." We learned that the refugee trail often begins with
conflict.

Several years later, while working in the Balkans as the war in Bosnia was nearing its end, we began to seriously grapple with forced mi-

gration. We met refugees—Bosnians, mainly, but also Croatians and Serbians—forced to escape their homes due to war. Some were nearly killed; many had lost family members. "All wished they could return home. But they couldn't. One man had fled his home in Bosnia with his wife and his accordion. Although he had lost everything else, including family members, he remained hopeful that someday he could rebuild his life. His accordion became his means to earn a living."[4]

Understanding the causes of forced migration permanently changed my perspective on refugees, including refugee resettlement. The heroes were the refugees themselves, who endured impossible odds not only to survive but also to help their family members and neighbors. Yet refugees today are routinely stigmatized or labeled "dangerous" because of the climate of fear created by terrorism. Moreover, those seeking to help them often find themselves labeled as theologically liberal, a code word for heretical or unpatriotic. Sometimes refugees or those helping them are even threatened. Last year someone left a voice message for one of my colleagues at World Relief saying he hoped my colleague and his family would die in the same way terrorists were killing Christians in the Middle East.

When you take a risk by doing the right thing, you will face criticism. Risk and persecution go hand in hand. History proves it, and so do our current times.

HAPPY ARE THE INSULTED

Jesus was a heretic turned hero. In his Sermon on the Mount, after uttering seven of the most sublime statements in all of Scripture, he concluded with his most daunting one: "Blessed are those who are persecuted because of righteousness, for theirs is the kingdom of heaven."⁵ Perhaps because he knew how ominous this sounded to his listeners, Jesus lessened the blow by promising a reward:

> Blessed are you when people insult you, persecute you and
> falsely say all kinds of evil against you because of me. Rejoice
> and be glad, because great is your reward in heaven, for in the
> same way they persecuted the prophets who were before you.⁶

Some people say that insults, slander, and persecution are an indication that we are doing something right. Others chalk them up to spiritual warfare or broken humanity. Such explanations can be comforting during hard times, but they also can be used to justify actions that are incongruent with the values Jesus taught. Sifting through our motives and actions to determine what really qualifies as persecution can be a difficult, but not impossible, exercise. Consider a scenario in which you've taken a stand on something underappreciated or controversial. Defending the rights of the unborn, alleviating poverty, ending labor or sex trafficking, stopping violence against women, or welcoming refugees comes to mind. First, ask yourself whether your issue is something Jesus wants his followers to care about. Then ask yourself whether your involvement with this issue is consistent with the values of Jesus's Great Sermon. Are you taking this stand in humility, mercifully, with empathy, with meekness, as a peacemaker, and so on? Mother Teresa, Dietrich Bonhoeffer, and Martin Luther King Jr. are good examples to look to in this regard. If you can answer yes to these questions *and you are still being insulted,* then you are likely being persecuted for righteousness, not personality or pride. You are siding with Jesus.

Happy are the insulted.

TO BE HUMAN IS TO SAY NO

Why do people tend to resist, reject, and even fight against doing the right thing? One reason may be that we tend to separate our personal faith from our public lives. That was true of me for a long time. For years I believed the problems of the world were outside the scope of my faith. I thought I was responsible for becoming personally righteous but not for seeing justice done in the world.

This dualism is only one reason for holding back, however. Theologians and pastors sometimes say that our sin nature is blind to injustice. I often meet God-fearing, moral people—including friends and neighbors, even family members and colleagues—who resist righteousness without realizing it. We've seen this phenomenon time and again throughout history. Christ followers endorsed slavery in the nineteenth century, apartheid in the twentieth, and HIV/AIDS as a form of divine punishment in the twenty-first.

Science can lend a helping hand in understanding this phenomenon. It seems we are hardwired to reject new things, including new things that are good or moral. Kevin Ashton, MIT professor, inventor of "the Internet of Things," and author of *How to Fly a Horse,* points out that the brain—specifically, the hippocampus, which serves an important role in processing information—works five hundred times faster in familiar situations than in new situations. In sum, our brains

work more efficiently when we're on familiar ground. The hippocampus is directly connected to an important nerve center, the amygdalae,
that drive our emotions. So we also feel better when things stay the
same, even if they are dead wrong. Ashton wrote:

> We swerve from what feels bad to what feels better. When
> something is new, our hippocampus finds few matching
> memories. It signals unfamiliarity to our amygdalae, which
> gives us feelings of uncertainty. Uncertainty is an aversive state:
> we avoid it if we can.[7]

Our tendency to crave sameness is furthered by our fear of rejection. For many of us, rejection, along with its expressions of loneliness
or, worse, abandonment, represents our deepest fear. Psychologists have
proven that babies will die without expressions of love, usually physical
touch. In his famous paper called "The Nature of Love," psychologist
Harry Harlow concluded that physical contact is even more important
than food. "We would rather die hungry than lonely," said Kevin
Ashton.[8] Even Mother Teresa, who fought the effects of physical disease
her whole life, called the "greatest disease . . . being unwanted, unloved,
and uncared for."[9]

A sense of belonging is a paramount psychological need for all
people.

When we bring together this fear of rejection and our natural tendency to resist anything new, we gain insight into why standing up for
justice is no small endeavor. It goes against our basic psychological, and
even biological, urges.

So how can we expect to counter these prevailing winds to create change?

THAT OTHER *F* WORD

In many ways the Bible is a collection of stories and principles that show us how to overcome fear with faith. The Bible contains countless examples of people standing for righteousness when everyone else shrank away in fear. You can name many of them: Noah building the ark, Moses defying Pharaoh, David standing against Goliath, Joshua toppling the walls of Jericho, and Mary believing the words of Gabriel. Peter, one of Jesus' disciples, exhibited both faith and fear, sometimes almost simultaneously. Jesus called him the rock, yet he also proved to be a coward when he publicly denied knowing Jesus, not just once but three times.

In one extraordinary account Jesus invited Peter to join him while walking on water:

When the disciples saw him walking on the lake, they were terrified. "It's a ghost," they said, and cried out in fear.

But Jesus immediately said to them: "Take courage! It is I. Don't be afraid."

"Lord, if it's you," Peter replied, "tell me to come to you on the water."

"Come," he said.

Then Peter got down out of the boat, walked on the water and came toward Jesus. But when he saw the wind,[10] he was afraid and, beginning to sink, cried out, "Lord, save me!"

Immediately Jesus reached out his hand and caught him. "You of little faith," he said, "why did you doubt?"

And when they climbed into the boat, the wind died down. Then those who were in the boat worshiped him, saying, "Truly you are the Son of God."[11]

Jesus called for courage from everyone in the boat—all the disciples were there—but only Peter mustered the gumption to respond. Maybe, like Peter, you would have risen to the challenge. Or maybe you are more risk averse, like the other disciples who conveniently deferred to "the rock" and let Peter's spontaneity get the best of him.

If you were in the boat, would you have leaped to your feet for the chance to walk on water? "I believe there is something—Someone—inside us who tells us there is more to life than sitting in a boat," wrote John Ortberg. "You were made for something more than merely avoiding failure. There is something inside you that wants to walk on the water—to leave the comfort of routine existence and abandon yourself to the high adventure of following God."[12]

Sometimes we must settle for nothing less than doing "the thing we think we cannot do," a phrase attributed to Eleanor Roosevelt, who lived a life filled with crises, both public and personal.

So why is it so hard to take risks? Our fear of rejection is closely linked with the fear of what some call the other *F* word—*failure*.[13] For many people failure is *the* most deeply rooted fear. Most of us have felt it to some degree, along with the fear of rejection we so closely associate with failure. And once we're rejected, shame typically settles in. Ortberg warned, "Failure in our day often carries with it shame—the shame not just of having experienced failure, but of *being* a failure. And facing this feeling is one of the hardest things a human being can do."[14]

Despite our near-phobic fear of failure, the facts suggest that it's actually a common, almost universal, experience:

- 75 percent of venture-capital-backed start-ups fail, and 95 percent do not meet the initial expectations.
- 40 percent of CEOs don't last eighteen months.
- 70 to 90 percent of mergers and acquisitions fail to add shareholder value.
- 81 percent of new hires don't work out.
- 99 percent of new patents never earn a penny.
- 95 percent of new products introduced in a given year fail.
- 68 percent of information technology projects fail to meet their goals.
- 88 percent of New Year's resolutions end in failure.
- 100 percent of all human bodies fail.[15]

It seems Alexander Pope was right when he said, *"Errāre hūmānum est,"* (to err is human).[16]

But did Peter *really* fail? Not long after his failure on the Sea of Galilee, Jesus asked Peter a question:

"Who do you say I am?"

Simon Peter answered, "You are the Messiah, the Son of the living God."

Jesus replied, "Blessed are you, Simon son of Jonah, for this was not revealed to you by flesh and blood, but by my Father in heaven. And I tell you that you are Peter, and on this rock I will

build my church, and the gates of Hades will not overcome it. I
will give you the keys of the kingdom of heaven."[17]

How could Jesus congratulate Peter for his faith after having just
admonished him for the lack of it? Maybe Peter's epic venture on the
water wasn't so much a failure after all.

Someone asked Winston Churchill what most prepared him to
lead Great Britain's fight against Nazi Germany. Churchill said it was
the time he had to repeat a grade in elementary school. "You mean you
failed a year in grade school?" he was asked. "I never failed anything in
my life," Churchill said. "I was given a second opportunity to get it
right."[18]

About his many unsuccessful attempts at creating the light bulb,
Thomas Edison said, "I have not failed. I've successfully found 10,000
ways that don't work."[19]

What if Peter's failure to surf the waves was merely preparation for
his future success? When "Peter puts himself in a position to fail,"
wrote Ortberg, "he also puts himself in a position to grow."[20]

In the end failure is not failure at all unless . . .

We give up.

Several years ago Belinda and I attended a spring concert where our
youngest son, Caleb, was slotted to perform a famous orchestral piece
with his fellow classmates. For months Caleb had practiced the drum
parts in our basement. Our whole family was familiar with each bass
ka-boom and snare-drum paradiddle. Ever the proud father, I embarrassed myself by standing to take photos during the event, reaching
over others to maximize my position for capturing stills and video clips.

The crowd—not just Belinda and I—roared with applause when the orchestra hit the last note.

Caleb had done an outstanding job.

When we all met up back at home, I expected Caleb to be in a celebratory mood like the rest of us. Smiling, I asked him how he felt about his performance. But Caleb's eyes were fixed downward, his voice demure, his expression sullen. "Dad, I feel terrible. I came in too early on one part," he said, "and I missed another part altogether. I totally let down my friends."

"No, Caleb," I said. "You were tremendous! Remember, I am a drummer too, and I didn't notice any mistakes. And if I didn't notice anything—"

"But, Dad," he interrupted, "I know where I messed up." Perplexed by his perspective, I asked him if he would be willing to watch the video clip.

"Dad, honestly, I don't want to relive my mistakes."

"Just try it; do it for me," I said. "You might be surprised."

Caleb reluctantly took my phone, sauntered down the hallway, and closed the door to his room. I could hear the clip play, then silence. He played it again, then silence. After a few minutes he came back into my office.

"Dad, it's really good!" he said. "I couldn't hear my mistakes at all!" His posture was open now, his joy ablaze. "Can you send me a copy?" he asked.

Afterward I sat back in my chair, relieved, pleased. My joy returned. But then these words began throbbing inside my head:

Stephan, you do this to yourself every day.

Um . . . wow. No, it can't be true.

Really?

Ouch.

Yes, yes, and yes. I fixate on my mistakes and internalize rejection (real or perceived) and sometimes shame too, while others—God included—see an entirely different reality.

God's videos are much different from ours.

LEAP OF FAITH

So who had more faith, Peter or his friends in the boat?

In his book *Scary Close: Dropping the Act and Finding True Intimacy,* Donald Miller wrote, "Those who can't accept their imperfections can't accept grace." Miller described how he learned to experience grace not because of, but through, his mistakes:

> I'd have to trust that my flaws were the ways through which I
> would receive grace. We don't think of our flaws as the glue that
> binds us to the people we love, but they are. Grace only sticks to
> our imperfections.[21]

I think he's right. The people who demonstrate the most grace are also the ones who freely speak about the lessons they've learned. If, then, there is no grace without mistakes (or at least no understanding of grace), and if there is no genuine faith without grace (as we noted in chapter 2), then there is no genuine faith without risk.

And grace will give us plenty of chances to take risks.

Peter took risks; he made a lot of mistakes. His faith grew, and he became, according to his Lord, the poster child for faith, the "rock" upon which the church was built.[22]

So what converted Peter the coward to Peter the rock? How do we, like Peter, overcome the overwhelming fear of rejection and stand against the crowd?

In the final chapter of John's account of the life of Jesus, we find Peter absolutely dejected. After denying his Lord and friend, Peter had all but given up. He'd returned to the only thing he knew: fishing. When Peter saw Jesus, now resurrected, on the shore preparing food, Peter plunged into the water, fully clothed, and swam to meet him. Peter's first words to Jesus aren't recorded. Was he overwhelmed by his friend's presence? Did he grovel? Apologize profusely? Weep?

We'll never know. But John recorded what happened next:

When they had finished eating, Jesus said to Simon Peter, "Simon son of John, do you love me more than these?"

"Yes, Lord," he said, "you know that I love you."

Jesus said, "Feed my lambs."

Again Jesus said, "Simon son of John, do you love me?"

He answered, "Yes, Lord, you know that I love you."

Jesus said, "Take care of my sheep."

The third time he said to him, "Simon son of John, do you love me?"

Peter was hurt because Jesus asked him the third time, "Do you love me?" He said, "Lord, you know all things; you know that I love you."

Jesus said, "Feed my sheep. Very truly I tell you, when you were younger you dressed yourself and went where you wanted;

but when you are old you will stretch out your hands, and
someone else will dress you and lead you where you do not want
to go." Jesus said this to indicate the kind of death by which
Peter would glorify God. Then he said to him, "Follow me!"[23]

Peter tried to go it alone and failed miserably. Out of cowardice,
Peter failed three times. With three questions Jesus reinstated Peter, not
with guilt or shame—the tools of fear—but with love. From that moment on, Peter was changed. Love restored him; love compelled him so
much that he was no longer held captive by his insecurities, his guilt, his
shame, and his fear. The love of God fired courage so deeply into Peter's
soul that it carried him through a flurry of epic experiences, from preach-
ing to thousands (Acts 2) to suffering with his fellow saints (1 Peter) to,
according to legend, being crucified upside down in Rome.

Peter's risk-taking led him to places he'd never dreamed of going.
Love converted Peter. Love can convert us too.

In his book *If You Want to Walk on Water, You've Got to Get Out
of the Boat,* John Ortberg asked a salient question: What is your boat?
He concluded,

Your boat is whatever represents safety and security to you apart
from God himself. Your boat is whatever you are tempted to put
your trust in, especially when life gets a little stormy. Your boat
is whatever keeps you so comfortable that you don't want to give
it up even if it's keeping you from joining Jesus on the waves.
Your boat is whatever pulls you away from the high adventure
of extreme discipleship.[24]

What risk will you take? You might consider

- stepping out within your career with an idea, a significant goal, or a new position — or pursuing a new career altogether,

- displaying vulnerability in a relationship by being fully honest, confessing wrongs, and asking forgiveness,

- admitting a weakness and boldly seeking advice, counsel, or help for an issue or problem, or

- committing to giving at a whole new level, in either money or time, which may take you way outside your comfort zone.

Perhaps your risk involves taking a stand. Maybe you will stand up for the refugee or immigrant. Or maybe you will confront the consumerism that has invaded your church and caused it to fit in rather than stand apart from the culture at large.

Remember: when you take a risk, it won't go perfectly well. Expect people to resist by actively pushing back, subtly insulting you, or not giving you the time of day. Remain humble, forgive freely, and follow Jesus by persevering in grace and truth. And don't trust the version of reality that plays in your head; instead watch God's video.

Peter is the poster child for failure but also our best example of the kind of faith upon which God can stake his plan. If you and I sometimes feel like failures and fear rejection, then both of us are in good company.

Name your boat. Step out of it. Move beyond your fear and into authentic faith. That's where the power is.

Nine

Defying Despair

A religious [person] . . . holds God and man in
one thought at one time, at all times, who suffers
harm done to others, whose greatest passion is
compassion, whose greatest strength is love and
defiance of despair.

—Abraham Joshua Heschel

In the aftermath of the 2010 earthquake in Haiti, hundreds of thousands of people died as a result of the seismic shock that shook the country.[1] Arriving in Port-au-Prince within hours of the quake, I grappled with overwhelming nausea as I met mothers and fathers who had lost children—and children who had lost mothers and fathers, brothers and sisters.

But I also encountered astonishing risk amid the unfathomable despair. The international response arrived late, but Haitians conducted their own search-and-rescue operations within communities while churches offered food, water, and shelter to thousands. One woman dove across the fragile, tender body of her two-year-old child just as her house began to collapse, her body shielding him from certain death. She died; he survived.

Love is the reason we risk.

WHAT MATTERS MOST

At the heart of faith is love, and at the heart of love is risk. God governs the universe accordingly. But he doesn't just require faith, love, and risk from us while he stands aloof. He personally showed the way and still does. By taking unprecedented risks, both Jesus and the apostle Paul presented and embodied the essence of faith, in its simplest terms, as love. Moses gave ten commandments; Jesus reduced them to just two—love God and others.[2] Paul named only one: "For the entire law is fulfilled in keeping this one command: 'Love your neighbor as yourself.'"[3]

Then why is faith so complicated? Maybe it's because we find it easier to follow a set of rules than to live by a bold principle. Maybe it's so hard to *really* love that we settle for things we can measure—filling pews, growing budgets, pursuing accolades. Maybe it's because reducing faith to its barest essential turns the pecking order completely upside down. Or maybe love is just too risky, too costly. Risk requires vulnerability, which exposes us to pain, which produces fear. Maybe we're just too afraid of getting hurt.

One of the great crescendos in Scripture comes when the apostle Paul says, "The only thing that counts is faith expressing itself through love."[4] If it were just faith or just love, it would be far easier. Faith would be reserved for ritual or ceremony, intellectual pursuits, social interaction, or "spiritual" journeys—all devoid of the messiness associated with love. That version of faith, so prevalent today, is aloof, sentimental, esoteric, or even superstitious. Faith without love seems safer, which is why so many prefer it. Yet that kind of faith draws fire in Scripture, as well it should. Jesus's brother James said, "Faith without deeds is dead."[5]

But love without faith is equally dangerous. Humanistic love can masquerade as the real thing and is sometimes necessary for temporarily holding together our bruised world. But such love cannot ultimately change us or others. Nor does it contain the power to overcome the world's deepest problems.[6] An either/or solution will never do. We need a both/and solution—both faith and love. Faith expressing itself in love is God's elegant solution to the problems we face.

THE REAL DEAL

Faith expressing itself in love is both liberating and exhilarating. Stripping faith from its excesses, extricating it from fear, leaves us feeling bare, raw, and vulnerable. The best we can bring to one another is our own vulnerability, as a sacrifice, an offering, a visible expression of invisible grace. From this place of transparency, of voluntary exposure, emerges something beautiful, something holy—real faith, free from the accoutrements of religion, cleansed of the desire for self-protection, liberated from the pecking order. It's only in this place of shared acceptance and vulnerability, "when we present our authentic, imperfect selves to the world" where "true belonging happens," wrote Brené Brown.[7]

Take a deep breath. Can you feel the burdens falling away? Can you sense your fear dissolving under the warmth of real, honest faith?

Though it is increasingly rare in the Western church, faith expressing itself in love is alive and well throughout the world. Often it is
tucked away in the least likely corners of the earth, not totally hidden
but not well publicized either. It is accessible to the sojourner who hun-
gers and thirsts for the real thing.

One of those corners of the world is Cambodia. Several years ago
when Belinda and our two sons said good-bye to our friends in Kigali,
Rwanda, a country where we had lived for nearly two years, we chose to
fly home the long way—through Asia. A day after arriving in Phnom
Penh, the capital of Cambodia, we drove beyond the frenetic city,
through a patchwork of rice paddies, to a cluster of villages about an
hour away.

A group of smiling children led us up the wooden steps of a home,
one of many sandwiched between a busy marketplace and the local
dump. Inside, on a pristine plank floor covered with intricately woven
carpets, we met three children, their parents, and a radiant grandmother. Smiling, we told them that our Rwandan friends instructed us
to "greet them with our teeth." As we did, the room lit up with laughter,
each person returning the favor. The grandmother drew attention to
her mouth, her smile displaying only a single tooth! We all joined in
another round of laughter.

After the exchange of greetings, we sang songs in Khmer. Someone
read the Bible. We listened as they told stories about their work to help
stem the spread of AIDS in their village, and we prayed together.

Then a woman in her thirties quietly slipped through the open
door. She had come from a friend who was sick with HIV. She told us
that she had administered medicine two days before. Then she began
to cry. "I visited her again last night, but she was getting worse. All I

could do was pray," she said. "I am late because I have just come from her. Today she is talking and walking! I am so happy." Tears streamed down her face as she proclaimed, "God healed her!"

You may have heard about the suffering of Cambodia's twelve million people. Their country's child-mortality rate is alarmingly high, as is the prevalence of HIV and AIDS. Most Cambodians live in rural areas with inadequate access to education, clean water, financial services, or medical care. Buddhism shapes the social, political, and cultural life of Cambodia.[8]

Years ago some friends in Cambodia pioneered a community banking initiative, which developed into a financial institution serving in excess of thirty-five thousand families. In its early days, when parents gathered in groups to borrow money or repay their loans, their children had nothing to do. So one of our staff members started a community health project for children. As she taught the children about their health, they asked her questions about her faith. Their health significantly improved, and many children chose to follow Jesus. Their parents began to ask why their children were so much better off. They, too, wanted to experience Jesus. So my colleagues organized small groups where the adults could gather to talk about faith and try to live out their new beliefs by loving their neighbors. The groups multiplied, giving way to a movement called Way of Hope.

Today the movement comprises roughly ten thousand people, organized into more than a thousand house churches, reaching out to children and families in more than a hundred villages in five provinces. Its members emphasize prayer and worship, local leadership, child participation, and service. Volunteer leaders do not, as a rule, have a high level of education. Some are illiterate. Participation, storytelling, and interactive methods are used to overcome this barrier. Members meet underneath homes built on stilts:

> For us, church means a group of people in the community where people can meet, can talk about God's Word—not only on Sunday. So our church is that we want them to come together, five people or ten people. Our church is a church with no walls.[9]

My Cambodian friends taught me something essential about church, community, and change. To this day I reflect often on those lessons. Church, for them, is not merely a tool for serving the poor and oppressed. They believe the church itself is also the goal. They see it as "in constant need of repentance and conversion" to become all it is meant to be.[10] Their groups of fifteen or so people are tiny communities of hope, incarnating the presence of God amid the pressing problems of rural Cambodia.

This is faith expressing itself in love.

Way of Hope emphasizes both word and deed in their communities, not merely alongside each other but integrated and interdependent.[11] To be a member is to worship, and to worship is to reach out. The leadership of this movement consists largely of lay people, both male and female. Very few of the leaders are formally trained for ministry, but they are deeply engaged in the community. By moving beyond the typical male-female and clergy-laity dichotomies, Way of Hope groups are able to empower those who are both closest to the needs and feel most called to serve.

My Khmer friends don't work "on behalf of" the poor. Instead, they invite the poor to become their own agents of change,[12] creating greater ownership and therefore greater sustainability.

A few years ago some of my former colleagues from World Relief took several visitors to the Kandal Province of Cambodia, about an hour's drive south of Phnom Penh. In one remote area the village chiefs were monitoring the changes that had taken place there. They said, "Since Jesus came to our villages, our children are healthier, AIDS-affected families are being cared for, there are fewer community problems, and people are getting along with each other better."[13]

I confess that I am often drawn to well-known people and organizations. They are inspiring and appear to be on the cutting edge and well resourced. Some of them are celebrities. Most such organizations are led by exceptional people—persuasive, insightful, and well-connected leaders, some of whom are friends of mine. I am indebted to them. Yet I have learned more from people like my friends in Cambodia. They remind me of the essence of faith. Way of Hope is not known by many outside of Cambodia. Yet God continues to accomplish miraculous things through the passion and faith of this beautiful group of people. They have no buildings to speak of, except the network of thousands of small homes. Their budget is small, and there are no famous names among them. They live on what we may consider the edge of the world. But what we call the edge, God often calls the center.

Just as it happened in Galilee in the first century, these Khmer disciples are inspiring thousands of people, including me, who long for a renewed vision of faith and church, in a world increasingly thirsty for the real thing. Following Jesus is not ultimately about resources or education or even theology, as useful as those things may be. It is about taking risks to live out the presence, values, and truth of Jesus, together, in community. It is faith expressing itself in love.

Are You the One?

Though there are many bright corners of the world where hope is astoundingly alive, there are also many problems. Despair seems ever present, always ready to pounce on the vulnerable.

In the early days of Jesus's life on earth, his cousin, John the Baptist, lost hope. But before we question John, remember that Jesus said of John, "Among those born of women there is no one greater."[14] Imprisoned, John sent a couple of disciples to ask Jesus some really hard questions. They said:

> "John the Baptist sent us to you to ask, 'Are you the one who is
> to come, or should we expect someone else?' " . . .
>   So he replied . . . , "Go back and report to John what you
> have seen and heard: The blind receive sight, the lame walk,
> those who have leprosy are cleansed, the deaf hear, the dead are
> raised, and the good news is proclaimed to the poor."[15]

A journalist once questioned me about the injustice caused by religion throughout history. "What if we were to count the dead bodies stacked up throughout history in the name of God?" he asked. "What about the slave trade, the thirty years' war following the Reformation, the Inquisition, the Crusades, the church being late to address the HIV/ AIDS crisis?"

"Could we also count the missing bodies?" I responded. "What if

Africa's suffering had never 'arrested' William Wilberforce's heart? What if a young girl from Albania had never listened to a call to serve the dying in India? What if Desmond Tutu had never lain his body across a white man about to be stoned by an angry mob? What if Jesus Christ had never taken upon himself the violence of the world so that one day all violence would cease? How many bodies would be stacked up then?" I asked.[16]

In reflection, my response was a bit pompous. Perhaps it was a sound argument, but I wonder if his question was as much personal as historical or theological. In the face of suffering, it's normal to question God.

Amid the wounds of the world, your own suffering, your over-whelming disappointment, seasons of confusion, unfulfilled promises, boredom, broken relationships, the marriage that's not going as well as you hoped, the child who is treading a dangerous path, the depression that nags at your soul—do you ever lose heart? In the quiet place in your heart, do you ever ask of God, *Are you really the one . . . , or . . .*

Even John the Baptist, the esteemed cousin of Jesus, the great prophet, asked, "Are you the one who is to come, or should we expect someone else?"

God has a way of answering our most desperate questions with seemingly simple statements in return: "Eat something" to Elijah. "Come and see" to the disciples. "Feed my sheep" to Peter. And here, to the disciples of John the Baptist, he said, "Report to John what you have seen and heard." Then he pointed to a surprising group of people living a radical promise with relentless faith. The blind see, the lame walk, those who had leprosy are clean, the deaf hear, the dead live, and the good news is proclaimed to the poor. As it turns out, Jesus had promised a similar version of hope a year or so earlier, when he announced his mission to neighbors and friends in Nazareth:

> The Spirit of the Lord is on me,
>> because he has anointed me
>> to proclaim good news to the poor.
> He has sent me to proclaim freedom for the prisoners
>> and recovery of sight for the blind,
> to set the oppressed free,
>> to proclaim the year of the Lord's favor.[17]

Unfortunately, those who heard this had a hard time accepting Jesus's version of faith. They ran him out of town instead.[18]

When it comes to faith, we tend to measure impact by proxy, numbers usually—people, money, buildings, or other numerical features associated with a strong brand. Instead, Jesus pointed to the riffraff and the miracles happening among them. Even John the Baptist, perhaps his earliest follower, was surprised and, we trust, encouraged by Jesus's criteria for success.

Why did Jesus point to the least of these as a litmus test for his mission? Maybe it was to demonstrate that if God can accomplish his purposes in the hardest of places, he can do it the world over. Or maybe God's power is stronger where people are more desperate. Either way, we must shift our gaze away from what we consider the center and follow Jesus to the periphery. Wisdom is found there. God himself is found in these most unlikely places, among the people who, because of their circumstances, tend to be more hungry and thirsty for him than others in less difficult circumstances.

While genuine fruit is sometimes more visible on the periphery, it is on full display for all who have eyes to see it. If the "least of these" are invited to experience grace, then we are too. That is the message. Nicodemus, the powerful Pharisee, and the Roman centurion mentioned in the Gospels understood this. They saw something on display on the margins of their society that they could not dismiss. They sought it out, and they found the presence of God, literally. They were changed as a result.

Because of the kind of work I do, people often ask me how I overcome the despair associated with suffering. Actually, I encounter profound hope in places of despair, and I find wisdom there—wisdom to help me live in a culture of decadence riddled with fear. Many people find it hard to believe hope can be found in unlikely places. This paradox can only be understood when we seek wisdom on the periphery, which I believe is actually the center stage of God's action.

Defying despair can become a way of life. If you haven't tried it, I beg you to take a risk.

BLESSED ARE THOSE WHO DON'T GIVE UP

The panoply of teachers we've encountered throughout our journey have, I hope, been inspiring. You too may have encountered wisdom from unlikely sources throughout your life. Reflecting on such wisdom through the lens of the Beatitudes is a tangible way to follow Jesus. In his Sermon on the Mount, he was signaling a revolutionary shift in how we see, understand, and pursue faith.

But where do we go from here? Can we continue to learn from the least of these even as we seek to live out our faith in breakthrough ways?

In many ways our journey has just begun. And for the challenges we face, there is joy too. "Only Jesus Christ, who bids us follow him, knows the journey's end," wrote Bonhoeffer. "But we do know that it will be a road of boundless mercy. Discipleship means joy."[19]

As you contemplate your next steps, consider the ideas below, or create your own. What matters most is that you don't give up but, instead, continue to "press on to take hold of that for which Christ Jesus took hold of" you.[20]

Blessed are the poor in spirit, for theirs is the kingdom of heaven. Pursue the "inversion" principle (Chapter 1: "Truth Furiously Knocking") by intentionally creating space to learn from the least of these. For example, do a live interview at your church with a refugee family; create a video featuring an African, Asian, or Hispanic leader changing her community; or cowrite an article for your school newspaper showcasing how someone from the so-called edge has shared surprising wisdom with you.

Blessed are those who mourn, for they will be comforted. Convene a group at your church, school, or office to view and discuss Chimamanda Ngozi Adichie's TED Talk "The Danger of a Single Story." Then interview a foreign-exchange student, immigrant, or refugee to understand that person's story from multiple perspectives (Chapter 3: "Kissing the Crucible"). Mourn with stories that are traumatic and celebrate stories of joy.

Blessed are the meek, for they will inherit the earth. Consider the felt needs in your home, school, or community. Then plan and carry out a postmodern foot washing (Chapter 4: "Divine and Dusty"), maybe with a few friends, your book club, or your study group.

Blessed are those who hunger and thirst for righteousness, for

they will be filled. Set aside some time each day, however brief, to pursue a conversational relationship with God (Chapter 6: "Break Open the Sky"). Be like Brother Lawrence: don't just talk or pray but listen with anticipation. As you do, you might consider reading through Dallas Willard's *Hearing God* as a resource.

Blessed are the merciful, for they will be shown mercy. Find a way to spend time with someone who represents a "sociological impossibility" (Chapter 5: "Wing Tips and Flip-Flops") in your community, school, or neighborhood. In your time together, pursue Henri Nouwen's "poverty of mind" by setting aside your opinions, assumptions, and judgments in order to understand another's perspective. Assume a "poverty of heart" by setting aside any worries, jealousies, and prejudices.[21]

Blessed are the pure in heart, for they will see God. Consider how you might tangibly "will the one thing" (Chapter 6: "Break Open the Sky") in a relationship with a family member, friend, colleague, child, girlfriend or boyfriend, or spouse by committing and demonstrating a new version of radical love through simple, selfless deeds.

Blessed are the peacemakers, for they will be called children of God. Consider an issue or cause that will require you to take a risk (Chapter 7: "Learning to Fly"). Set aside some time for research—talk to friends, read, pray, lament, or visit organizations or ministries focused on the issue or cause—and set yourself a goal for taking a tangible risk. You might begin by talking about the issue or cause with friends, family, and colleagues. You might be an advocate of your cause with your local officials or politicians. Or you might join an exposure/learning trip.

Blessed are those who are persecuted because of righteousness, for theirs is the kingdom of heaven. Write a letter to yourself giving your best wisdom on how you plan to respond to future failure, challenge, or persecution. Ask yourself whether you have been consistent with the values of Jesus's Great Sermon: humility, empathy, mercy, meekness, purity, peacemaking, and so on. Tell yourself never to give up, because perceived failures are actually an investment in future success. Then put your letter in an envelope, seal it, write "The Other *F* Word" across it, and save it for *that* day (Chapter 8: "Heretics and Heroes").

EASTER IS A VERB

As of late it feels as though the world is hurtling toward narcissism, nihilism, and despair. In the face of such challenges, the world laughs at namby-pamby faith, moralism, and sentimental religion. It scoffs at well-intentioned do-gooders, justifying its cynicism by referring to the bickering and infighting of the church.

Ouch.

But the world cannot laugh when the sick are healed, the lame walk, the deaf hear, and the dead are raised to life. When we follow Jesus into streets and alleyways, dusty villages and urban sprawls, office complexes and university campuses, he does extraordinary things through people like you and me.

A friend of ours, Edith from Togo, once raised a man from the dead. Really? Come on. Yet Edith tells the story with such vivid detail, humility, and unfeigned conviction, I cannot doubt her story. In a village in Africa, she was asked to pray for a man who had died, but she was reluctant to do so. Afraid, she tried to escape the situation but tripped as she turned to leave and found herself partially sprawled across the dead man's body. In utter desperation she prayed that God would raise him from the dead.

God did, the man arose, and Edith lived to tell the story.

Dr. Gary is a friend who lives and works with Mercy Ships, a ship-based hospital serving people in places with woefully inadequate health care. Dr. Gary has performed maxilofacial surgery on thousands of people with tumors, most of whom would have died without intervention. During one screening in West Africa, thousands of people, most of them desperate for help, came in hopes they'd make the list to receive a surgery. Eventually Dr. Gary was forced to choose between two young boys, both with life-threatening tumors about the same size. Dr. Gary had already maxed out the surgery schedule, committing his team to a grueling rotation, including late nights. He paused, turned away from the families seeking his help, said a brief prayer, and made a choice. Before informing the boy's family that their son would not receive surgery, Dr. Gary placed his hands upon their child and prayed that God would heal him somehow.

Months later, as the first boy was recovering in the shipboard hospital ward, Dr. Gary was asked to meet with a family who had come to visit him. It was the family of the boy Dr. Gary had declined to operate on. They presented their son, whose tumor had miraculously disappeared, and thanked Dr. Gary for praying for him.

It doesn't stop there. Friends from Washington DC just returned from a trip to India where they witnessed scores of healings. Miracles are more common than we think.

Maybe we shouldn't be so surprised. After all, Jesus's mission was to overcome death—not just his own but ours too. Easter is the holiday that celebrates this overcoming. Its symbols—the cross, the empty grave, lilies, even baby chicks—all allude to the power of life over death. Our word *Easter* is etymologically linked to the Hebrew word *pesach,* or Passover (*pascha* in Greek translation). In the Hebrew narrative, death "passed over" the Israelites during their escape from Egyptian oppression. Jesus has become the new pascha, causing death, in all its manifestations—physical, spiritual, social—to pass away.

Easter commemorates the end of death, the liberation from ultimate despair, the certain "sting"[22] that plagues all humanity. At Easter, death throws up its feeble arms and surrenders itself to life. Little boys with tumors live to grow old. Young girls are rescued from modern-day slavery. Rotten scoundrels give their lives to God and become kindhearted souls.

Easter is not just a holiday. It is God's means of awakening the world from despair. Easter has the potential to convert ceremonial, sentimental, or superstitious faith into the real thing. Easter is, in fact, a verb:

> For the mother who trembles as she scrapes the last bite
> > for her hungry child? *Easter.*
> For the child who is stolen from her village and sold?
> > *Easter.*
> For the father who faces the daily shame of poverty?
> > *Easter.*
> For a people ravaged by violence and war? *Easter.*
> For our disappointments, our drudgery, our grief?
> > *Easter.*

Save us from our fickle, fragile selves, O God;
Pass over this broken earth.
Easter us

We pray.

As a verb, Easter is inclusive. It has the power to produce change in
all directions for all people, mutually and reciprocally. The benefactor
and beneficiary both need Easter; the oppressed and the opulent need
Easter; the well-intentioned and the "I never intended" need Easter.

We need Easter. We need it badly, and we need it every day.

Some friends of ours got into a discussion one day about faith. Tim
and Jay landed on the same question Jesus once entertained from a
lawyer: Who is my neighbor?

Tim decided to take up that question in prayer each day for thirty
days. For twenty-eight days, not much happened. Life carried on pretty
much as normal.

Until day twenty-nine.

On that day, an otherwise normal day, Tim's wife, Terri, went out
to get the mail only to find her mailbox in pieces, its wooden frame
strewed across the road. Stunned, she called the police, who came to
investigate. The officer told Terri that her mailbox had been destroyed
by one of her neighbors. How did he know? He had followed the pieces
of the mailbox along the road and up the driveway to a garage just two
houses down.

Tim and Terri live in an affluent neighborhood near Minneapolis.
Tim is a banker. Terri is a bioethicist. She speculated that the culprit
was a teenager venting anger or maybe an anti-bank protestor targeting

their home. Or perhaps alcohol had played a role. Terri was determined to learn more.

The police officer returned to tell her the situation was entirely different from what she expected. Terri's neighbor had hit her mailbox with her car. She was a first-generation immigrant, lonely and scared. She had fled her home country of Uganda, where she had been tortured, her family threatened, and her husband and brothers killed by the Lord's Resistance Army. She had come to the United States to seek asylum, leaving her three children behind with her mother and extended family in hopes that she could establish a life here and bring her kids later. She had found work in the home two doors down, taking care of the elderly homeowner in exchange for room, board, and a stipend.

The immigrant woman's name was Harriet.

Harriet trembled when she met Tim and Terri and promised to pay for the mailbox. Tim is a first-rate leader, banker, and visionary whose presence can be intimidating, but he's actually one of the kindest souls I know. When Tim and Terri told Harriet that she didn't need to worry about the mailbox and that they were just grateful no one was hurt, Harriet knelt and prayed for them both, blessing them for "their forgiveness."

Tim and Terri didn't charge Harriet for the damages. Instead, they helped her buy a new car because hers was severely damaged in the accident. They later assisted her in bringing her children to the United States and began a friendship with Harriet that fundamentally changed their lives. "I've never known anyone as wise, brave, and daily reliant on God," said Terri. "She is my ultimate role model."

When the couple began to understand the plight of immigrants and refugees, they traveled to Africa and immersed themselves in finding innovative solutions to poverty. Tim joined the board of one organization focused on protecting the most vulnerable, and Terri joined another.

All because of Harriet.

Who would have thought that Harriet, among the most vulnerable herself, coming from a war-torn area on the fringe of the planet with seemingly little to offer, would become the teacher of a well-to-do, highly educated power couple living at the center of the so-called first world?

God is "precisely . . . present via those who are the absent," said one theologian.[23] So often we look for Easter in the wrong places. Yet when we find it, despair evaporates and we are changed.

Jesus sparked change from a corner of the world that was marginal, if not immaterial, in his day. From that unlikely starting point, he pulled together a motley group of followers having few resources and changed the course of history. He pointed to the poor, hungry, mournful, and merciful as prime examples of his proposed way of life, the kingdom of God, as he called it.

And God is still calling our attention away from the superficial aspects of life to the real thing. What we consider the edge, God calls the center. He asks us to follow him there, to take a risk, to love, to defy despair, so that we can join him in bringing Easter here, now, whether to the person across the desk, the refugee who wrecked your mailbox, the church that has lost its first love, the school that needs a new start, or the community where people have thrown their hands up in despair.

Easter us, we pray, so we can rise to sing healing songs to broken bones, so we can take that elusive risk and defy that impossibility and shatter the fearful cage that still traps our trepid souls. Easter us so we can genuinely learn to give and receive authentic love and so we can, together, break open the sky.

Don't Be Afraid

We are made for larger ends than Earth
can encompass.
Oh, let us be true to our exalted destiny.
—Catherine Booth

We live in perilous times, but just how perilous is debatable. Some threats are real, others only perceived. Our political, social, and spiritual discourse feels urgent regardless of the vying perspectives. Many say racial tensions are at an all-time high, while others say it's always been this way.

Whether threats are real or perceived, each of us feels the psychological stress. Fear is palpable.

Some are predicting the demise of Western hegemony—politically, militarily, and culturally. Others believe Western society is still strong but in need of a significant course correction. Some say the moral fiber of our nation is at risk. Most believe we are facing a tipping, or turning, point: we can choose to become a better society, or we can recede from significance. How we respond matters, maybe now more than ever.

The stakes are high.

The reasons for our predicament vary depending on whom you ask. In politics, conservatives blame liberals, and liberals blame conservatives. Within the faith community, progressives blame fundamentalists, and fundamentalists blame progressives. At a macro level, secularists blame religion, and religious people blame secularism. I wonder if all our blaming is actually an exercise in futility.

I believe those of us who follow Jesus face an even more fundamental dilemma, one deeper than our differences in politics, culture, or even theology. We face a crisis of identity, a question that affects the soul of our community and our witness to the world at large. We are experiencing a referendum on our faith, whether we realize it or not. We are being forced to answer the most basic questions about who we are as followers of Jesus. Will we surrender the heart of our faith to the vulture of fear, which hovers over the ailing body of the church? Or will we reject fear as our organizing principle and rediscover the bold faith delivered to us by Jesus himself, a faith that expresses itself with extravagant love?

The world is watching closely to see what we will do.

In reference to the never-ending rhetoric in the public square, much of which reverberates in our pubs, coffee shops, churches, and on social media, a friend said, "There are too many words."[1] Regarding politics? True. Few would disagree. Regarding our culture? Likely true as well.

But what about our faith? Christianity is a religion of the Word. Words—truths expressed in language—are central to who we are. So in one sense our words matter, and they matter a lot. We cannot step back from Scripture or from expressing its truths.

On the other hand, I wonder what would become of our faith if we were to talk less and live more? Enacting the simple principles Jesus preached in his Great Sermon is a good place to start. But such ideas are far from simple when we translate them into life. Let's face it, it's far easier to preach or blog or write a book(!) about the Beatitudes than it is to live them.

What if we were to get serious about becoming poor in spirit, thirsty for righteousness and justice, impassioned for peacemaking, and absolutely merciful? What if we didn't fight back when persecution came near? What if we were to talk less and listen more to our heroic friends on the margins?

If we did, we might be surprised by the outcome of that referendum on our faith.

When I think about the people who have impacted my life, I usually don't think of people who are eloquent, possess expertise, or command the attention of thousands. I think about people who are largely unknown but who have taught me how to forgive, how to love, how to risk for the sake of others. They are unsung heroes and heroines. Their theology is unsophisticated, but they live the simple truths they believe. Their choices are not made for show but are motivated by convictions forged in the crucible of sorrow. They accept their suffering even as they resist it, without considering themselves entitled to a comfortable life. Their demeanor is marked by gratitude, even joy, often for simple things. They offer hope and beauty amid the drudgery that accompanies daily life and human need: working the land, preparing food, raising kids, singing, walking, praying. This is the farmer who kneels on his rented land and offers a simple prayer for rain and then rises to his feet with a kind of trust that many of us will never know. This is the mother of four whose calloused hands scour the earth for meager bits of protein to feed her children, never giving in to despair. This is the young woman who reaches for the heavens to survive another day while retrieving her dignity from the floor, having been discarded there by men whose deeds are too evil to name.

I am not describing a version of faith that is separate from orthodoxy. No, this version of faith is, if anything, more orthodox than the sentimentality or dogmatism we commonly accept. I am speaking of grace that redeems absolutely, thoroughly, irrevocably, through one Savior; repentance that relinquishes self, surrendering fully to a countercultural kingdom; and love that abandons itself to God, that both gives and forgives, that always trusts, always perseveres, always hopes, and that takes risks surprising enough to break open the sky.

Frederick Buechner said, "Here is the world. Beautiful and terrible things will happen. Don't be afraid."[2] So often we expect someone else to change the things that we know are desperately in need of reformation. And in one sense it's quite natural to think there are better people than us to tackle such grand projects. But over and over again history tells of common folk, people like our friends on the other side of the world or down the street, people like you and me who take small steps of faith. I am convinced it is these unlikely souls who end up changing the world.

God's history books differ from ours.

As you take these risks, good things will come your way; you can be sure of that. But you can be equally sure hard times will test your resolve. Remember this, however: if you persevere, the hard times will forge in you a new faith, a bold faith, an indispensable faith, strong enough to astonish you, strong enough to course correct a church or a community or even a nation. Rest assured, an ocean of grace awaits any who dare to dip a toe. Don't be afraid. It's time to unlace those wing tips, kick off those flip-flops, and plunge both feet onto the dusty path that beckons you.

Stephan Bauman

January 1, 2017

Acknowledgments

To all those who embody authentic faith in our post-truth culture of fear, thank you, dear prophets and poets for showing us the way. A special thanks to David Burnham, for living the life of faith without the superfluous talk. To Bill Haley and Coracle for oozing faith and confronting the superficiality in me now, then, and still to come. To Andy, Sunita, Gabe, Addie, and our goddaughter, Asha, thank you for personifying the community of Christ within your home and family. You are infinitely and unconditionally loved. To Don and Brenda Jacobson, thank you for being true, real, and always visionary. Our love and gratitude. To Lynne Hybels, thank you for being a forerunner to so many and never giving up. To David, Tina, and fam, yep, you guys are the real deal. Thank you for loving us in spite of. To JB, Roanna, Manita, and Kennedy, thank you for loving us without claim, so gracefully, so freely. To the Reddys, thank you for the benefit of the doubt. To the Klinepeters, you guys got it going on. Thanks for pursuing it, not that. To the Welker and Traudt clan, in-laws too! Nothing compares with being with you all on the road—let's do it again. To David Neff and Jason Poling, you guys are prototyping the essence of church, Whistle Pig style, for many and for me—stay fearless. To Jason Ferenczi, for wearing your heart on the outside of your chest, even as you outthink all of us. Thank you Ron, Ken Kregel, Brent Fearon, Katie Sytsma, Steve Mayer, Kristin, David, Tim, Sara, Joel, Adam, and Angie for leaning hard into him. To the Gordon fam—what can I say but thank you for the honor and example.

To Joe and Steph Johns, Andrew Hoffman, Becky, and the crew at FMC. You betcha, your vision is his, and we want to make it ours. To Wytsma and the rest, don't stop. You keep inspirin' us. To Micah B., keep on teachin' us and loving us as white as we can sometimes be. To Quinn, we're on your turf in 2017. Thanks for being reckless with love. To the Vander Kolks, thank you for rolling out the red carpet and to David Stoner and Scott Gustafson for including us in your wild and wondrous world. To Ruth and Jeff, we'll follow you. Just tell us where and when. To Cyprien, Zeburia, and fam, you remain a North Star to which we look to see the sky. To Paul Borthwick, thanks for always choosing grace (and wit!). To John and Noel Gichinga, you both display and exude grace and love in extraordinary ways. Thank you for leading by example. To Gil and Elmarie Odendaal, we love you both. To the Garrels, thank you for blasting sublime holes in heaven's doors. Don't stop, ever, young prophet man. To Marcel and the DRC crew, we are yours. Just say the word. Thank you JP and Clementine, *nos amours le vôtre.* To Nicholas Hitimana, don't stop. We are your cheerleaders. To Bob Oehrig and Arrive Ministries (www.arriveministries.org) for the Somali story and to Jill Myer for the Scary Close tip. To David Kopp, Andrew Stoddard, and the entire Multnomah WaterBrook team: without you, these words would fall flat. To Mom, Dad, Chris, and Phil Wilson, we love you to our dying day. To Mom and Dad Bauman, ditto; thank you for pouring your souls into us. To Frank, Rita, and kids, and Pam, our love, and to Brenda, still *Selah.* To my sons, Joshua and Caleb, now friends and purveyors of wisdom so young, so soon. I am always in your court, always your champion. To B., the one who stole my love so many years ago. *Je t'aimerai toujours.* And to the One who stole my life once and for all, *Soli Deo Gloria,* again and always.

Notes

Introduction: Disillusioned

1. Joseph Akwiri, "Passenger Says Muslims Protect Christians in Islamist Attack on Kenyan Bus," Reuters, December 21, 2015, www.reuters.com /article/us-kenya-attacks-somalia-idUSKBN0U41LD20151221.
2. "Kenyan Muslims Shield Christians in Mandera Bus Attack," BBC News, December 21, 2015, www.bbc.com/news/world-africa-35151967.
3. Elahe Izadi and Sarah Kaplan, "Muslims Protect Christians from Extremists in Kenya Bus Attack," *Washington Post,* December 22, 2015, www .washingtonpost.com/news/acts-of-faith/wp/2015/12/22/muslims -protected-christians-from-extremists-in-kenya-bus-attack-reports-say/.
4. Matthew 25:40; 5:44.
5. Barna Group, *Barna Trends 2017: What's New and What's Next at the Intersection of Faith and Culture* (Grand Rapids, MI: Baker, 2017), 150.
6. David Brooks, "The Epidemic of Worry," *New York Times,* October 25, 2016, www.nytimes.com/2016/10/25/opinion/the-epidemic-of-worry .html?_r=0.
7. Neil Strauss, "Why We're Living in the Age of Fear," *Rolling Stone,* October 6, 2016, www.rollingstone.com/politics/features /why-were-living-in-the-age-of-fear-w443554.
8. "Black Lives Matter and Racial Tension in America," Barna: Research Releases in Culture and Media, May 5, 2016, www.barna.com/research /black-lives-matter-and-racial-tension-in-america/#.
9. Emma Lazarus, "The New Colossus" (1883), written to raise money for the construction of the pedestal of the Statue of Liberty and inscribed inside the pedestal's lower level.
10. Matthew 25:35–37.
11. Sheri Ledbetter, "America's Top Fears 2015" (blog), Wilkinson College of Arts, Humanities, and Social Sciences, Chapman University, October 13, 2015, https://blogs.chapman.edu/wilkinson/2015/10/13 /americas-top-fears-2015/.

12. S. A. Miller, "Homeland Insecurity: Americans Feel Less Safe Than Any Time Since 9/11, Poll Finds," *Washington Times,* September 10, 2014, www.washingtontimes.com/news/2014/sep/10 /america-feel-more-unsafe-anytime-911-ready-militar/.

13. "Most Expect 'Occasional Acts of Terrorism' in the Future," Pew Research Center, April 23, 2013, www.people-press.org/2013/04/23 /most-expect-occasional-acts-of-terrorism-in-the-future/.

14. "New Fox Poll shows 54% favor temporarily banning Non-U.S. muslims," Fox News, Twitter post, March 23, 2016, https://twitter.com /FoxNews/status/712770755889508352.

15. Daniel Gardner, *The Science of Fear: How the Culture of Fear Manipulates Your Brain* (New York: Penguin, 2008), 5–6. Ironically, when Eleanor Roosevelt was asked to comment on her husband's inauguration, she referred to it as "terrifying!"

16. Max Roser, "Life Expectancy," Our World in Data, https://ourworldindata .org/life-expectancy/.

17. "Life Expectancy," Global Health Observatory (GHO) data, World Health Organization, www.who.int/gho/mortality_burden_disease/life_tables /situation_trends/en/.

18. "Achievements in Public Health, 1900–1999: Healthier Mothers and Babies," Centers for Disease Control, October 1, 1999, www.cdc.gov /mmwr/preview/mmwrhtml/mm4838a2.htm.

19. "Poverty Overview," World Bank, October 2, 2016, www.worldbank.org /en/topic/poverty/overview.

20. C. S. Lewis, "The Inner Ring," C. S. Lewis Society of California, www .lewissociety.org/innerring.php.

21. New World Encyclopedia Online, s.v. "William Temple," www .newworldencyclopedia.org/entry/William_Temple.

22. See Isaiah 55:1.

23. Niccolo Machiavelli, *The Prince,* trans. N. H. Thomson, The Harvard Classics, vol. 36 (New York: Collier & Son, 1909–14), www.bartleby .com/36/1/17.html.

24. In reference to the first account of sin in the book of Genesis.

25. Anyone reading this book is likely in the top 1 percent globally. See, for example, Charles Kenny, "We're All the 1 Percent," Foreign Policy, February 27, 2012, http://foreignpolicy.com/2012/02/27 /were-all-the-1-percent/.

26. See Graeme Wood, "Secret Fears of the Super-Rich," *Atlantic,* April 2011, www.theatlantic.com/magazine/archive/2011/04 /secret-fears-of-the-super-rich/308419/.

27. Brooks, "Epidemic of Worry," www.nytimes.com/2016/10/25/opinion
/the-epidemic-of-worry.html?_r=0.
28. Don Otis, "Anxiety Disorders and Phobias on the Rise: Women More
Susceptible to Stress than Men," Christian NewsWire, April 26, 2011,
www.christiannewswire.com/news/8460116831.html.
29. For example, well-known Boston sociologist Peter Berger said that by
"the 21st century, religious believers are likely to be found only in small
sects, huddled together to resist a worldwide secular culture." (See Peter
Berger, "A Bleak Outlook Is Seen for Religion," *New York Times,* April
25, 1968.)
30. Rodney Stark, *The Triumph of Faith: Why the World Is More Religious
than Ever* (Wilmington, DE: ISI Books, 2015), 2.
31. In 2015 the Pew Research Center shared its findings that "the percentage
of adults (18 and older) who describe themselves as Christians has dropped
by nearly eight percentage points in just seven years," while the "religiously
unaffiliated," people who self-identify as atheists, agnostics, or "nothing in
particular," comprise 22.8 percent of the US adult population. (See
"America's Changing Religious Landscape," Pew Research Center, May
12, 2015, www.pewforum.org/2015/05/12/americas-changing-religious
-landscape/; and Michael Lipka, "A Closer Look at America's Rapidly
Growing Religious 'Nones,'" Pew Research Center, May 13, 2015, www
.pewresearch.org/fact-tank/2015/05/13/a-closer-look-at-americas-rapidly
-growing-religious-nones/.)
32. Stark, *Triumph of Faith,* 2.
33. Matthew Rose, "Tayloring Christianity," *First Things,* December 2014,
www.firstthings.com/article/2014/12/tayloring-christianity.
34. See, for example, Mark Oppenheimer, "The Evangelical Scion Who
Stopped Believing," *New York Times Magazine,* December 29, 2016,
www.nytimes.com/2016/12/29/magazine/the-evangelical-scion-who
-stopped-believing.html?smprod=nytcore-ipad&smid=nytcore-ipad-share.
35. Charles Taylor, *A Secular Age* (Cambridge, MA: Harvard University Press,
2007), 430.
36. Dallas Willard, *The Spirit of the Disciplines: Understanding How God
Changes Lives* (San Francisco: HarperOne, 1999), xii.
37. "60 Minutes/Vanity Fair Poll: Fear," CBS News, January 5, 2015, www
.cbsnews.com/news/60-minutesvanity-fair-poll-fear/.
38. Dietrich Bonhoeffer, *The Cost of Discipleship* (New York: Touchstone,
1959), 37–38.
39. See Matthew 5:14–15.
40. Walter Mosley, *Blue Light* (New York: Little, Brown, 1998), 277.

Chapter 1: Truth Furiously Knocking

1. Hilary Holladay, *Wild Blessings: The Poetry of Lucille Clifton* (Baton Rouge: Louisiana State University Press, 2012), 39.
2. "Oxford Dictionaries: Word of the Year," Oxford Dictionaries, https:// en.oxforddictionaries.com/word-of-the-year/word-of-the-year-2016.
3. This definition comes from David Mikkelson, the founder of Snopes, the myth-busting website, and was quoted in Jeremy W. Peters, "Wielding Claims of 'Fake News,' Conservatives Take Aim at Mainstream Media," *New York Times,* December 25, 2016, www.nytimes.com/2016/12/25/us /politics/fake-news-claims-conservatives-mainstream-media-.html.
4. Art Swift, "Americans' Trust in Mass Media Sinks to New Low," Gallup, September 14, 2016, www.gallup.com/poll/195542/americans-trust-mass -media-sinks-new-low.aspx.
5. "Speech by John Adams at the Boston Massacre Trial," Boston Massacre Historical Society, www.bostonmassacre.net/trial/acct-adams3.htm.
6. *The New Strong's Expanded Dictionary of Bible Words* (Nashville, TN: Thomas Nelson, 2001), 1315, s.v. *"pistis."*
7. Hebrews 11:1, KJV.
8. John 14:6.
9. See John 8:32.
10. Stephan Bauman, Matthew Soerens, Issam Smeir, *Seeking Refuge: On the Shores of the Global Refugee Crisis* (Chicago: Moody, 2016), 2.
11. Karen Miller Pensiero, "Aylan Kurdi and the Photos That Change History," *Wall Street Journal,* September 11, 2015, www.wsj.com/articles /aylan-kurdi-and-the-photos-that-change-history-1442002594.
12. Until recently the US Office of Refugee Resettlement, though perhaps not widely understood, generally enjoyed bipartisan support in Congress and drew criticism only from a small segment of Americans. Yet by early 2016, just over half of the US population favored keeping refugees out of our country. Even ministers shared this perspective. For example, Franklin Graham said, "For some time I have been saying that Muslim immigration into the United States should be stopped until we can properly vet them or until the war with Islam is over." (See Sarah Larimer, "Why Franklin Graham Says Donald Trump Is Right About Stopping Muslim Immigra- tion," *Washington Post,* December 10, 2015, www.washingtonpost.com /news/acts-of-faith/wp/2015/12/10/why-franklin-graham-says-donald -trump-is-right-about-stopping-muslim-immigration/?utm_term= .3b10019cfca4.) Others are more hostile. At a public meeting in a South Carolina high school cafeteria, one critic called for refugees to be deported

or, if that was not possible, shot. (See Richard Fausset, "Refugee Crisis in Syria Raises Fears in South Carolina," *New York Times,* September 25, 2015, www.nytimes.com/2015/09/26/us/refugee-crisis-in-syria -raises-fears-in-south-carolina.html.)

13. 1 John 3:16.

14. Jonathan Merritt, "Saint Fred," *Atlantic,* November 22, 2015, www .theatlantic.com/politics/archive/2015/11/mister-rogers-saint/416838/.

15. Fred Rogers, address to Boston University Convocation, 1992 (video), Fred Rogers Beyond the Neighborhood, http://exhibit.fredrogerscenter.org /advocacy-for-children/videos/view/971/.

16. Fred Rogers, Commencement Address, Middlebury College, Middlebury, Vermont, May 2001, www.middlebury.edu/newsroom/commencement /2001.

17. The people of Jesus's time would have learned about God from the Torah, which is the first five books of the Bible (the Pentateuch), and from the Talmud, an oral tradition explaining the Torah.

18. See Matthew 5:19–20.

19. John 3:9–10, 12.

20. George Weigel, "Franciscan Churchmanship," *First Things,* January 2017, 46.

21. John 1:10.

22. *Oxford English Dictionary,* s.v. "revelation," https://en.oxforddictionaries .com/definition/revelation.

23. John 9:39.

24. Dallas Willard, *The Divine Conspiracy: Rediscovering Our Hidden Life in God* (San Francisco: HarperSanFrancisco, 2009), 98.

25. Willard, *Divine Conspiracy,* 100.

26. Willard, *Divine Conspiracy,* 102.

27. John Stott and Martyn Lloyd-Jones, to name two.

28. Matthew 6:10.

29. The word *Anaw* in Hebrew means both poverty and softness. The two words in Hebrew, *ani* and *anu,* from the root *anah,* mean "to be humbled, afflicted, lowered." These terms originate from the root *nh,* meaning "the decline with inferiority," while *ani* means "poor bent, lowered . . ." (Glossary of Hebrew Scripture, http://hebrascriptur.com/Lexolive/xpauvre.html).

30. John Ortberg, "Dallas Willard, a Man from Another 'Time Zone,'" *Christianity Today,* May 8, 2013, www.christianitytoday.com/ct/2013 /may-web-only/man-from-another-time-zone.html.

31. See Hebrews 11:1.

32. John 3:17, nrsv.

Chapter 2: A Banana Peel for the Orthodox Foot

1. Roko Belic, *Happy,* directed by Roko Belic (New York: Wadi Rum Productions, 2011), www.thehappymovie.com/film/.
2. Hans Villarica, "Maslow 2.0: A New and Improved Recipe for Happiness," *Atlantic,* August 17, 2011, www.theatlantic.com/health/archive/2011/08 /maslow-20-a-new-and-improved-recipe-for-happiness/243486/.
3. Villarica, "Maslow 2.0," www.theatlantic.com/health/archive/2011/08 /maslow-20-a-new-and-improved-recipe-for-happiness/243486/.
4. Daryl Collins et al., *Portfolios of the Poor: How the World's Poor Live on $2 a Day* (Princeton, NJ: Princeton University Press, 2009), Kindle location 1685–87.
5. United Nations, "Happiness Should Have Greater Role in Development Policy—UN Member States," UN News Centre, July 19, 2011, www .un.org/apps/news/story.asp?NewsID=39084#.VxtOApMrKRs.
6. Katia Hetter, "Where Are the World's Happiest Countries?" CNN, March 21, 2016, www.cnn.com/2016/03/16/travel/worlds-happiest-countries -united-nations/.
7. Keith Breene, "The World's Happiest Countries in 2016," World Economic Forum, www.weforum.org/agenda/2016/11/the-worlds-happiest -countries-in-2016/.
8. Sabrina Tavernise, "U.S. Suicide Rate Surges to a 30-Year High," *New York Times,* April 22, 2016, www.nytimes.com/2016/04/22/health/us-suicide -rate-surges-to-a-30-year-high.html?_r=0.
9. Elizabeth Cohen, "CDC: Antidepressants Most Prescribed Drugs in U.S.," CNN, July 9, 2007, www.cnn.com/2007/HEALTH/07/09/antidepressants /index.html.
10. Sharon Jayson, "The Goal: Wealth and Fame but 'The Good Life' Could Elude Gen Y," *USA Today,* January 10, 2007, http://usatoday30.usatoday .com/educate/college/firstyear/articles/20070114.htm. See also Alice G. Walton, "Millennial Generation's Non-Negotiables: Money, Fame and Image," *Forbes,* March 19, 2012, www.forbes.com/sites/alicegwalton /2012/03/19/millennial-generations-non-negotiables-money-fame-and -image/#e7022784faad.
11. Nancy Gibbs, "One Day in America," *Time,* November 15, 2007, http:// content.time.com/time/specials/2007/article/0,28804,1674995 _1683300_1683301,00.html.
12. Chukwuma Muanya, "Why Nigerians, Ghanaians, Mexicans, Columbians Are Among Happiest People on Earth," *Guardian,* January 22, 2016, http://guardian.ng/news/why-nigerians-ghanaians-mexicans-columbians -are-among-happiest-people-on-earth/.

13. Dallas Willard, *The Divine Conspiracy: Rediscovering Our Hidden Life in God* (New York: HarperCollins, 2008), 100.
14. Willard, *Divine Conspiracy,* 101.
15. Willard, *Divine Conspiracy,* 102.
16. Ephesians 2:8–9.
17. Social and Demographic Trends, "Millennials in Adulthood," Pew Research Center, March 7, 2014, www.pewsocialtrends.org/2014/03/07 /millennials-in-adulthood/.
18. R. R. Reno, "Crisis of Solidarity," *First Things,* November 2015, www .firstthings.com/article/2015/11/crisis-of-solidarity.
19. To be sure, the deity of Christ, incarnation, and atonement are all essential to our salvation. By emphasizing grace as the key truth for living a vibrant faith, I don't intend to underappreciate the full range of essential theological truth.
20. Joe Pinsker, "Why So Many Smart People Aren't Happy," *Atlantic,* April 26, 2016, www.theatlantic.com/business/archive/2016/04 /why-so-many-smart-people-arent-happy/479832/.
21. Robert Farrar Capon, *Between Noon and Three: Romance, Law, and the Outrage of Grace* (Grand Rapids, MI: Eerdmans, 1997), 7.
22. Matthew 20:1–16.
23. Luke 15:11–32.
24. John Blase, "Brennan Manning: All Is Grace: God Loves You as You Are," *Huffington Post,* December 28, 2011, www.huffingtonpost.com /john-blase/all-is-grace-god-loves-you-as-you-are_b_1030799.html.
25. Matthew 5:6, TLB.
26. Brennan Manning and John Blase, *All Is Grace: A Ragamuffin Memoir* (Colorado Springs, CO: Cook, 2011), 194.

Chapter 3: Kissing the Crucible

1. Gordon Conway, *One Billion Hungry: Can We Feed the World?* (Ithaca, NY: Cornell University Press, 2012).
2. Didi Kirsten Tatlow, "27 Million People Said to Live in 'Modern Slavery,'" *New York Times,* June 20, 2013, https://rendezvous.blogs.nytimes.com /2013/06/20/27-million-people-said-to-live-in-modern-slavery/?_r=0.
3. Adrian Edwards, "Global Forced Displacement Hits Record High," UNHCR—UN Refugee Agency, June 20, 2016, www.unhcr.org/en-us /news/latest/2016/6/5763b65a4/global-forced-displacement-hits-record -high.html.
4. "100 Million Americans Have Chronic Pain," CBS News, April 19, 2012, www.cbsnews.com/news/100-million-americans-have-chronic-pain/.

5. C. S. Lewis, *The Horse and His Boy,* The Chronicles of Narnia (New York: HarperCollins, 2009), 163.

6. Henri J. M. Nouwen, *The Dance of Life: Weaving Sorrows and Blessings into One Joyful Step,* ed. Michael Ford (Notre Dame, IN: Ave Maria Press, 2006), 181.

7. Timothy Keller, *Walking with God through Pain and Suffering* (New York: Penguin, 2013), 16.

8. Keller, *Walking with God,* 42.

9. See, for example, Keller, *Walking with God,* 4–5.

10. Quoted in Timothy Keller, *The Reason for God: Belief in an Age of Skepticism* (New York: Dutton, 2008), 25.

11. Timothy Keller, Twitter, April 8, 2014, https://twitter.com/timkellernyc /status/453641213862637571.

12. Keller, *Walking with God,* 30.

13. Luke 23:34.

14. Peter Kreeft, "God's Answer to Suffering," from Peter Kreeft, *Making Sense Out of Suffering* (Ann Arbor, MI: Servant, 1986), www.peterkreeft .com/topics/suffering.htm.

15. Matthew 5:4.

16. Bono, "Because We Can, We Must," Between Issues, *Almanac,* May 19, 2004, www.upenn.edu/almanac/between/2004/commence-b.html.

17. Chimamanda Ngozi Adichie, "The Danger of a Single Story," (video), TED Global, July 2009, www.ted.com/talks/chimamanda_adichie_the _danger_of_a_single_story#t-681083.

18. Luke 7:47.

19. Keller, *Walking with God,* 49.

20. C. S. Lewis, *Mere Christianity,* Truth According to Scripture, www .truthaccordingtoscripture.com/documents/apologetics/mere-christianity /Book2/cs-lewis-mere-christianity-book2.php#.WFw76LYrKRs.

21. See Matthew 6:12–13.

22. Aleksandr Solzhenitsyn, *The Gulag Archipelago, 1918–1956: An Experiment in Literary Investigation III–IV,* trans. Thomas P. Whitney (London: Harvill Press, 1974), 615; Aleksandr Solzhenitsyn, *The Gulag Archipelago, 1918–1956: An Experiment in Literary Investigation I–II,* trans. Thomas P. Whitney (London: Harvill Press, 1974), 168.

23. See Genesis 37–50.

24. Genesis 50:19–21.

25. See Stephan Bauman, *Possible: A Blueprint for Changing How We Change the World* (Colorado Springs, CO: Multnomah, 2015), 15–18.

26. Luke 13:4–5, ESV.
27. Often attributed to Fyodor Dostoyevsky, these words are said to be from an untitled poem (dated 1878) by the nineteenth century Russian poet Apollon Maykov. The full quatrain, in Russian, reads: "Не говори, что нет спасенья, / Что ты в печалях изнемог: / Чем ночь темней, тем ярче звезды, / Чем глубже скорбь, тем ближе Бог."
28. "Bono and Eugene Peterson on the Psalms" (video), Fuller Studio, https://fullerstudio.fuller.edu/bono-eugene-peterson-psalms/.
29. "Bono and Eugene Peterson," https://fullerstudio.fuller.edu/bono-eugene-peterson-psalms/.
30. Revelation 21:4, KJV.
31. Paraphrase of Isaiah 28:29, KJV.
32. Rajeshwari Subramaniam, *A Primer of Anesthesia* (New Delhi, India: Jaypee Brothers Medical Publishers, 2008), xxiii.

Chapter 4: Divine and Dusty

1. David J. Bosch, *Transforming Mission: Paradigm Shifts in Theology of Mission*, American Society of Missiology Series, no. 16, 20th anniv. ed., (Maryknoll, NY: Orbis Books, 2011), 380.
2. John 1:14.
3. *Strong's Exhaustive Concordance of the Bible*, s.v. skénoó (4637), Bible Hub, http://biblehub.com/greek/4637.htm.
4. "The Roman Empire in the First Century: Slaves and Freemen," PBS, www.pbs.org/empires/romans/empire/slaves_freemen.html.
5. Luke 1:52, 68, 71; 2:14.
6. Luke 1:32.
7. Philippians 2:6–8, ESV.
8. Michael J. Gorman, *Inhabiting the Cruciform God: Kenosis, Justification, and Theosis in Paul's Narrative Soteriology* (Grand Rapids, MI: Eerdmans, 2009), 26.
9. John Dominic Crossan and Jonathan L. Reed, *In Search of Paul: How Jesus's Apostle Opposed Rome's Empire with God's Kingdom* (San Francisco: HarperSanFrancisco, 2004), 290.
10. Henri J. M. Nouwen, *The Dance of Life: Weaving Sorrows and Blessings into One Joyful Step*, ed. Michael Ford (Notre Dame, IN: Ave Maria Press, 2005), 138–39.
11. Matthew 5:5.
12. *Strong's Exhaustive Concordance of the Bible*, s.v. praus (4239), Bible Hub, http://biblehub.com/greek/4239.htm.

13. Isaiah 29:14.
14. Michael Gerson, "The Children Among Syria's Ruins," *Washington Post,*
    October 15, 2015, www.washingtonpost.com/opinions/syrian-children
    -among-the-ruins/2015/10/15/8d0510de-7360-11e5-8d93-0af317ed58c9
    _story.html?utm_term=.30e80587495d.
15. Adrian Edwards, "Global Forced Displacement Hits Record High,"
    UNHCR—UN Refugee Agency, June 20, 2016, www.unhcr.org/en-us
    /news/latest/2016/6/5763b65a4/global-forced-displacement-hits-record
    -high.html.
16. See Deuteronomy 10:19 and Matthew 25:35, for example.
17. A bit of history and data can go a long way to assuage our concerns. The
    United States has resettled over three million refugees since the late 1970s.
    None have been terrorists. World Relief, the organization I previously served,
    has resettled nearly three hundred thousand refugees since 1978. None have
    been terrorists. There is good reason for this: the vetting process for refugees
    who qualify for resettlement is extensive. The FBI, the State Department,
    national intelligence agencies, and the Department of Homeland Security
    are all involved in a process that takes up to two years to complete and
    requires clearing a number of significant hurdles. Refugees are not the threat
    that some make them out to be. Also, refugees are a good investment. Many
    people believe that refugees are a burden to the countries that receive them,
    but the opposite is true. Studies show that welcoming refugees often has a
    positive effect on a host country's economy and wages. Germany is some-
    times referred to as the new "land of the free and the brave" because they are
    accepting around eight hundred thousand Syrians. While we applaud
    Germany's moral courage, it was also a smart move. The decision is as much
    economic as moral.
18. Interestingly, Eleanor Roosevelt said one of her greatest regrets was not
    helping more Jewish refugees enter the United States during WWII. See
    Jay Winik, *1944: FDR and the Year That Changed History* (New York:
    Simon and Schuster, 2015).
19. John 13:4–5.
20. John 13:14–15.
21. John 13:34–35.
22. Attributed to Francis Schaeffer.
23. "Ten Pieces of Wisdom from Desmond Tutu on His Birthday," Desmond
    Tutu Peace Foundation, October 7, 2015, www.tutufoundationusa
    .org/2015/10/07/10-pieces-of-wisdom-from-desmond-tutu-on-his
    -birthday/.

24. Brian Frost, *Struggling to Forgive: Nelson Mandela and South Africa's Search for Reconciliation* (London: Harper Collins, 1988), 41.
25. Michael Battle, *Reconciliation: The Ubuntu Theology of Desmond Tutu* (Cleveland: Pilgrim Press, 1997), 5.
26. B. J. de Klerk, "Nelson Mandela and Desmond Tutu: Living Icons of Reconciliation," *Ecumenical Review* 55, no. 4 (October 2003): 327, doi: 10.1111/j.1758-6623.2003.tb00467.
27. 1 Corinthians 12:26.
28. James 2:18, NIV 1984.

Chapter 5: Wing Tips and Flip-Flops

1. Mother Teresa, "Whatsoever You Do . . .": Speech of Mother Teresa of Calcutta to the National Prayer Breakfast, Washington, DC, February 3, 1994, Priests for Life, www.priestsforlife.org/brochures/mtspeech.html.
2. Bono, "Transcript: Bono Remarks at the National Prayer Breakfast," *USA Today,* February 2, 2006, www.americanrhetoric.com/speeches/bononationalprayerbreakfast.htm.
3. David Bosch, *Transforming Mission: Paradigm Shifts in Theology of Mission,* American Society of Missiology, no. 16 (Maryknoll, NY: Orbis Books, 2011), 49.
4. Ed Stetzer, quoted in Bryan Loritts, "The Most Segregated Hour of the Week?" (blog: The Exchange), *Christianity Today,* January 19, 2015, www.christianitytoday.com/edstetzer/2015/january/most-segregated-hour-of-week.html.
5. Philip Kariatlis, *Church as Communion: The Gift and the Goal of Koinonia* (Hindmarsh, Australia: ATF Press, 2011), 40.
6. Philippians 2:1–2.
7. Galatians 3:28.
8. Scot McKnight, *A Fellowship of Differents: Showing the World God's Design for Life Together* (Grand Rapids, MI: Zondervan, 2015).
9. D. A. Carson, *Love in Hard Places* (Wheaton, IL: Crossway, 2002), 61.
10. David Swanson, "Down with the Homogeneous Unit Principle?" *Christianity Today,* August 2010, www.christianitytoday.com/pastors/2010/august-online-only/down-with-homogeneous-unit-principle.html.
11. Tami Hoag, *Dark Horse* (New York: Random House, 2002), 65.
12. See John 3:16.
13. Matthew 5:7.
14. James 2:13.

15. Frederick Buechner, *Beyond Words: Daily Readings in the ABC's of Faith* (San Francisco: HarperSanFrancisco, 2004), 228–29.
16. Henri J. M. Nouwen, *Reaching Out: The Three Movements of the Spiritual Life* (Garden City, NY: Doubleday, 1986), 66.
17. Nouwen, *Reaching Out,* 66.
18. Nouwen, *Reaching Out,* 87–93.
19. John 14:6.
20. Galatians 2:20.
21. Matthew 11:28.
22. See John 14:26.
23. John 14:1, NLT.
24. Matthew 5:6.
25. Methodist Church in Britain, "A Covenant with God," www.methodist .org.uk/who-we-are/what-is-distinctive-about-methodism/a -covenant-with-god.

Chapter 6: Break Open the Sky

1. Emily Roenigk, "5 Reasons Poverty Porn Empowers the Wrong Person," ONE, April 9, 2014, www.one.org/us/2014/04/09 /5-reasons-poverty-porn-empowers-the-wrong-person/.
2. See chapter 9 of Stephan Bauman, *Possible: A Blueprint for Changing How We Change the World* (Colorado Springs, CO: Multnomah, 2015).
3. Katherine Boo, *Behind the Beautiful Forevers: Life, Death, and Hope in a Mumbai Undercity* (New York: Random House, 2012), 237.
4. Margaret Heffernan, "Forget the Pecking Order at Work" (video), TED, May 2015, www.ted.com/talks/margaret_heffernan_why_it_s_time _to_forget_the_pecking_order_at_work?language=en.
5. *Tsedeqah,* along with its root, *tsedeq,* is consistently translated *dikaiosu ne* in the Septuagint, the Greek translation of the Old Testament.
6. Some scholars, including Pope Francis, translate the verse as "Blessed are those who hunger and thirst for justice" to capture the relational dimension intended by Jesus.
7. Deuteronomy 6:4–5.
8. Matthew 19:19.
9. Matthew 22:36–40.
10. Galatians 5:14.
11. Carmen Acevedo Butcher, "The Limping, Unceasingly Praying Brother Lawrence," *Christianity Today,* September 2009, www.christianitytoday .com/history/2009/september/limping-unceasingly-praying-brother -lawrence.html.

12. "Brother Lawrence Biography," The Practice of the Presence of God, 2017, http://thepracticeofthepresenceofgod.com/brother-lawrence/.
13. Brother Lawrence, *The Practice of the Presence of God* (New Kensington, PA: Whitaker, 1982), Kindle location 436–37.
14. "Brother Lawrence: Practitioner of God's Presence," *Christianity Today,* www.christianitytoday.com/history/people/innertravelers /brother-lawrence.html.
15. Mark Woods, "Brother Lawrence, the Kitchen Saint: 10 Quotes from The Practice of the Presence of God," *Christian Today,* April 27, 2016, www .christiantoday.com/article/brother.lawrence.the.kitchen.saint.10.quotes .from.the.practice.of.the.presence.of.god/84927.htm.
16. Brother Lawrence, *The Practice of the Presence of God,* Kindle location 27–28.
17. Quoted in Dallas Willard, *Hearing God: Developing a Conversational Relationship with God* (Downers Grove, IL: InterVarsity, 2012), 17.
18. Willard, *Hearing God,* 20.
19. Willard, *Hearing God,* 26.
20. Kenneth L. Woodward, "Talking to God," *Newsweek,* January 5, 1992, www.newsweek.com/talking-god-197774.
21. Kathryn Jean Lopez, "America Has a Prayer," *National Review,* December 6, 2012, www.nationalreview.com/corner/334932 /america-has-prayer-kathryn-jean-lopez.
22. Willard, *Hearing God,* 21.
23. 1 Corinthians 13:1–13.
24. Michael Connelly, *The Last Coyote* (New York: Grand Central, 2013), 10.
25. Two words are used for *justice* in the Old Testament. The first, *mishpat,* means to render judgment or to give people what they are due. This is sometimes referred to as rectifying justice. The second word, *tsedeqah,* means the right thing or, especially, right relationships. This is referred to as primary justice. These words are often paired in Scripture as "justice and righteousness," and in some instances one means the other. See Bauman, *Possible,* 82.
26. Micah Bournes, "Is Justice Worth It?" www.micahbournes.com /videos/2016/9/2/is-justice-worth-it. Used with permission.
27. Matthew 5:8.
28. Søren Kierkegaard, "Purity of Heart Is to Will One Thing," Religion -Online.org, www.religion-online.org/showbook.asp?title=2523.
29. 1 John 4:11–16.
30. 1 John 4:18–19.
31. Augustine, *Confessions,* 1.1.1.

32. Often I ask myself whether my friends in the majority world are really more vulnerable than we are.

33. Galatians 5:1.

34. "Mother Teresa Quotes," www.betterworld.net/heroes/pages-t /teresa-quotes.htm.

35. 1 Corinthians 12:26.

36. Gordon Conway, *One Billion Hungry: Can We Feed the World?* (Ithaca, NY: Cornell University Press, 2012).

37. "Overview," World Bank, www.worldbank.org/en/topic/poverty/overview.

38. Jens Manuel Krogstad, Jeffrey S. Passel, and D'Vera Cohn, "5 Facts About Illegal Immigration in the U.S.," FactTank, Pew Research Center, November 3, 2016, www.pewresearch.org/fact-tank/2016/11/03 /5-facts-about-illegal-immigration-in-the-u-s/.

39. Didi Kirsten Tatlow, "27 Million People Said to Live in 'Modern Slavery,'" *New York Times,* June 20, 2013, https://rendezvous.blogs.nytimes.com /2013/06/20/27-million-people-said-to-live-in-modern-slavery/?_r=0.

40. Nicholas D. Kristof and Sheryl WuDunn, *Half the Sky: Turning Oppression into Opportunity for Women Worldwide* (New York: Knopf, 2009), ii.

Chapter 7: Learning to Fly

1. 1 Corinthians 12:26.

2. The name has been changed to protect his identity.

3. Matthew 17:20.

4. Hebrews 12:2.

5. Luke 7:36–50.

6. Michael Pritzl, "The Song of the Harlot," The Violet Burning, *Strength,* copyright © 1992.

7. Spiros Zodhiates, *The Complete Word Study Dictionary: New Testament* (Chattanooga, TN: AMG Publishers, 1992), "peacemaker."

8. Matthew 5:9.

9. Holland Lee Hendrix, "Jews and the Roman Empire," *Frontline,* PBS.org, April 1998, www.pbs.org/wgbh/pages/frontline/shows/religion/portrait /jews.html.

10. Bruce Bradshaw, *Bridging the Gap: Evangelism, Development and Shalom,* book 5 of Innovations in Mission (Monrovia, CA: MARC, 1993), 19.

11. Rob Morris, "Her Name Became a Number: Her Number Became Our Name," Love146, n.d., https://love146.org/love-story/.

12. Quote Investigator, "Jump Off the Cliff and Build Your Wings on the Way Down," http://quoteinvestigator.com/2012/06/17/cliff-wings/.
13. Oswald Chambers, "Yes—But . . . !" *My Utmost for His Highest*, May 30, https://utmost.org/classic/yes-but-classic/.
14. See 1 John 4:18.

Chapter 8: Heretics and Heroes

1. Ernie Harburg, "A Tribute to Blacklisted Lyricist Yip Harburg: The Man Who Put the Rainbow in The Wizard of Oz," Democracy Now!, December 25, 2015, www.democracynow.org/2015/12/25/a_tribute _to_blacklisted_lyricist_yip.
2. Alessandro Conti, "John Wyclif," *The Stanford Encyclopedia of Philosophy* (Spring 2017), ed. Edward N. Zalta, https://plato.stanford.edu/entries /wyclif/.
3. Elisabetta Povoledo, "Mother Teresa Is Made a Saint by Pope Francis," *New York Times,* September 3, 2016, www.nytimes.com/2016/09/05 /world/europe/mother-teresa-named-saint-by-pope-francis.html.
4. Stephan Bauman, Matthew Soerens, and Issam Smeir, *Seeking Refuge: On the Shores of the Global Refugee Crisis* (Chicago: Moody, 2016), 21.
5. Matthew 5:10.
6. Matthew 5:11–12.
7. Kevin Ashton, *How to Fly a Horse: The Secret History of Creation, Invention, and Discovery* (New York: Doubleday, 2015), 86.
8. Ashton, *How to Fly a Horse,* 86.
9. Mother Teresa, "Mother Teresa of Calcutta Quotes," Quotation Source, www.quotationsource.com/q-1965-The-greatest-disease-in-the-West .htm.
10. Squalls are not uncommon on the Sea of Galilee since the surrounding topography lends itself to sudden weather changes. The sea is nearly seven hundred feet below sea level. It is surrounded by hills, the steepest of which lie on its eastern shore. Coming through the hills, cool air reaches the valley and collides with warm air trapped over the water, producing volatile conditions.
11. Matthew 14:26–33.
12. John Ortberg, *If You Want to Walk on Water, You've Got to Get Out of the Boat* (Grand Rapids, MI: Zondervan, 2001), 17.
13. John Danner and Mark Coopersmith, *The Other "F" Word: How Smart Leaders, Teams, and Entrepreneurs Put Failure to Work* (Hoboken, NJ: Wiley & Sons, 2015), 15.

14. Ortberg, *If You Want to Walk on Water,* 141.
15. Danner and Coopersmith, *The Other "F" Word,* 22–23.
16. Alexander Pope, "An Essay on Criticism," *The Works,* www.ling.upenn .edu/courses/Fall_2003/ling001/pope_crit.htm.
17. Matthew 16:15–19.
18. Quoted in Ortberg, *If You Want to Walk on Water,* 22–23.
19. Quoted in Danner and Coopersmith, *The Other "F" Word,* 34–35.
20. Ortberg, *If You Want to Walk on Water,* 24.
21. Donald Miller, *Scary Close: Dropping the Act and Finding True Intimacy* (Nashville: Nelson, 2014), 45.
22. Matthew 16:18.
23. John 21:15–19.
24. Ortberg, *If You Want to Walk on Water,* 17.

Chapter 9: Defying Despair

1. Estimates range between 220,000 and 316,000 people. See CNN Library, "Haiti Earthquake Fast Facts," December 28, 2016, www.cnn.com/2013 /12/12/world/haiti-earthquake-fast-facts/.
2. Luke 10:27.
3. Galatians 5:14.
4. Galatians 5:6.
5. James 2:26.
6. From a theological perspective, humanistic love—the good done by people outside of any attribution to God—can be ascribed to common grace, the principle that all good is from God.
7. Brené Brown, *Daring Greatly: How the Courage to Be Vulnerable Transforms the Way We Live, Love, Parent, and Lead* (New York: Gotham, 2012), 145.
8. Only 2 percent of Cambodians are Christians.
9. Way of Hope provincial leader, interviewed by the author, Phnom Penh, Cambodia, September 2007.
10. See, for example, Brad Harper and Paul Louis Metzger, *Exploring Ecclesiology: An Evangelical and Ecumenical Introduction* (Grand Rapids, MI: Brazos Press, 2009). Also see David Bosch's discussion of *ecclesia semper reformanda* in David Bosch, *Transforming Mission: Paradigm Shifts in Theology of Mission* (Maryknoll, NY: Orbis Books, 1991), 453.
11. "Micah Network Declaration on Integral Mission," developed at the Micah Network Consultation on Integral Mission held in Oxford, England, September 27, 2001, www.micahnetwork.org/sites/default/files/doc/page /mn_integral_mission_declaration_en.pdf.

12. Too often well-intentioned outsiders seek to work for the poor or even with the poor, but in so doing they snuff out local initiative. Such a posture, along with its corresponding models, can further entrench poverty, especially the form of poverty that results when the beneficiary feels inferior rather than as a colleague. Bryant Myers, Jayakumar Christian, and others tackle this subject by identifying poverty of being and poverty of vocation as the deepest and worst forms of poverty. See Bryant L. Myers, *Walking with the Poor: Principles and Practices of Transformational Development* (Maryknoll, NY: Orbis Books, 1999).

13. Tim Amstutz, World Relief Country Director in Cambodia, interviewed by the author in September 2013, Phnom Penh, Cambodia.

14. Luke 7:28.

15. Luke 7:20, 22.

16. Stephan Bauman, *Possible: A Blueprint for Changing How We Change the World* (Colorado Springs, CO: Multnomah, 2015), 77.

17. Luke 4:18–19.

18. Luke 4:29.

19. Dietrich Bonhoeffer, *The Cost of Discipleship* (New York: Touchstone, 2012), 38.

20. Philippians 3:12.

21. Henri J. M. Nouwen, *Reaching Out: The Three Movements of the Spiritual Life* (New York: Doubleday, 1975). 86–87.

22. See 1 Corinthians 15:55.

23. Alexander Nava, *The Mystical and Prophetic Thought of Simone Weil and Gustavo Gutiérrez: Reflections on the Mystery and Hiddenness of God* (Albany, NY: State University of New York Press, 2001), 142.

Afterword: Don't Be Afraid

1. Malcolm Street, used with permission.

2. Frederick Buechner, *Beyond Words: Daily Readings in the ABC's of Faith* (San Francisco: HarperSanFrancisco, 2004), 139.

About the Author

Stephan Bauman is the executive director of a foundation serving the least resourced and accessible places of the world. Prior to working in philanthropy, Stephan served as president and CEO of World Relief, an international relief and development organization partnering with the global church to serve more than five million vulnerable people each year.

Stephan's pursuit of justice led him to leave a successful career in the Fortune 100 sector to live in Africa, where he directed relief and development programs for nearly a decade before returning to the United States. Stephan lives to see people everywhere rise to the call of justice and give their lives in ways that empower the least of these toward real change, a vision he continues to pursue. Stephan holds degrees from Johns Hopkins University, Wheaton College, and the University of Wisconsin. He is the author of two previous books: *Possible: A Blueprint for Changing How We Change the World* and *Seeking Refuge: On the Shores of the Global Refugee Crisis*.

Stephan considers his African friends his most important teachers, and his wife, Belinda, his most important mentor. Stephan, Belinda, and their two sons, Joshua and Caleb, live near Grand Rapids, Michigan, where they enjoy the woods, the arts, and late-night conversations with friends.

CHANGE YOURSELF.
CHANGE THE WORLD.

A STIRRING YET PRAGMATIC TREATISE ON HOW INDIVIDUALS AND CHURCHES CAN BE CATALYSTS FOR RADICAL, POSITIVE AND LASTING CHANGE.

LEARN MORE AT WATERBROOKMULTNOMAH.COM

MULTNOMAH